College of Wooster
Wooster, Ohio

Written by Sarah Core

*Edited by Kristen Burns, James Balzer, Kimberly Moore,
and Alyson Pope*

Layout by Adam Burns

*Additional contributions by Omid Gohari,
Christina Koshzow, Chris Mason, Joey Rahimi,
and Luke Skurman*

ISBN # 1-4274-0044-X
ISSN # 1551-9775
© Copyright 2006 College Prowler
All Rights Reserved
Printed in the U.S.A.
www.collegeprowler.com

Last updated: 5/15/06

√ISBN
college 378.73
COl

Special Thanks To: Babs Carryer, Andy Hannah, LaunchCyte, Tim O'Brien, Bob Sehlinger, Thomas Emerson, Andrew Skurman, Barbara Skurman, Bert Mann, Dave Lehman, Daniel Fayock, Chris Babyak, The Donald H. Jones Center for Entrepreneurship, Terry Slease, Jerry McGinnis, Bill Ecenberger, Idie McGinty, Kyle Russell, Jacque Zaremba, Larry Winderbaum, Roland Allen, Jon Reider, Team Evankovich, Lauren Varacalli, Abu Noaman, Mark Exler, Daniel Steinmeyer, Jared Cohon, Gabriela Oates, David Koegler, Glen Meakem, and the College of Wooster Bounce-Back Team.

College Prowler®
5001 Baum Blvd.
Suite 750
Pittsburgh, PA 15213

Phone: 1-800-290-2682
Fax: 1-800-772-4972
E-Mail: info@collegeprowler.com
Web Site: www.collegeprowler.com

How this all started...

When I was trying to find the perfect college, I used every resource that was available to me. I went online to visit school websites; I talked with my high school guidance counselor; I read book after book; I hired a private counselor. Sure, this was all very helpful, but nothing really told me what life was like at the schools I cared about. These sources weren't giving me enough information to be totally confident in my decision.

In all my research, there were only two ways to get the information I wanted.

The first was to physically visit the campuses and see if things were really how the brochures described them, but this was quite expensive and not always feasible. The second involved a missing ingredient: the students. Actually talking to a few students at those schools gave me a taste of the information that I needed so badly. The problem was that I wanted more but didn't have access to enough people.

In the end, I weighed my options and decided on a school that felt right and had a great academic reputation, but truth be told, the choice was still very much a crapshoot. I had done as much research as any other student, but was I 100 percent positive that I had picked the school of my dreams?

Absolutely not.

My dream in creating *College Prowler* was to build a resource that people can use with confidence. My own college search experience taught me the importance of gaining true insider insight; that's why the majority of this guide is composed of quotes from actual students. After all, shouldn't you hear about a school from the people who know it best?

I hope you enjoy reading this book as much as I've enjoyed putting it together. Tell me what you think when you get a chance. I'd love to hear your college selection stories.

Luke Skurman
CEO and Co-Founder
lukeskurman@collegeprowler.com

Welcome to College Prowler®

During the writing of College Prowler's guidebooks, we felt it was critical that our content was unbiased and unaffiliated with any college or university. We think it's important that our readers get honest information and a realistic impression of the student opinions on any campus—that's why if any aspect of a particular school is terrible, we (unlike a campus brochure) intend to publish it. While we do keep an eye out for the occasional extremist—the cheerleader or the cynic—we take pride in letting the students tell it like it is. We strive to create a book that's as representative as possible of each particular campus. Our books cover both the good and the bad, and whether the survey responses point to recurring trends or a variation in opinion, these sentiments are directly and proportionally expressed through our guides.

College Prowler guidebooks are in the hands of students throughout the entire process of their creation. Because you can't make student-written guides without the students, we have students at each campus who help write, randomly survey their peers, edit, layout, and perform accuracy checks on every book that we publish. From the very beginning, student writers gather the most up-to-date stats, facts, and inside information on their colleges. They fill each section with student quotes and summarize the findings in editorial reviews. In addition, each school receives a collection of letter grades (A through F) that reflect student opinion and help to represent contentment, prominence, or satisfaction for each of our 20 specific categories. Just as in grade school, the higher the mark the more content, more prominent, or more satisfied the students are with the particular category.

Once a book is written, additional students serve as editors and check for accuracy even more extensively. Our bounce-back team—a group of randomly selected students who have no involvement with the project—are asked to read over the material in order to help ensure that the book accurately expresses every aspect of the university and its students. This same process is applied to the 200-plus schools College Prowler currently covers. Each book is the result of endless student contributions, hundreds of pages of research and writing, and countless hours of hard work. All of this has led to the creation of a student information network that stretches across the nation to every school that we cover. It's no easy accomplishment, but it's the reason that our guides are such a great resource.

When reading our books and looking at our grades, keep in mind that every college is different and that the students who make up each school are not uniform—as a result, it is important to assess schools on a case-by-case basis. Because it's impossible to summarize an entire school with a single number or description, each book provides a dialogue, not a decision, that's made up of 20 different topics and hundreds of student quotes. In the end, we hope that this guide will serve as a valuable tool in your college selection process. Enjoy!

OMID GOHARI ◯ CHRISTINA KOSHZOW ◯ CHRIS MASON ◯ JOEY RAHIMI ◯ LUKE SKURMAN ◯
The College Prowler Team

COLLEGE OF WOOSTER
Table of Contents

Introduction from the Author

"So you're going to Woo-stur is it," people ask me constantly, drawling out the "oo" and grinning widely at the funny sound. "No, no," I insist, "It's Wu-ster." And yes, we are in the middle of Amish country. And yes, we are a very small liberal arts school that many people don't know about. And yes, we are continuing to produce well-rounded, independently-thinking people who go on to achieve wonderful things. After all, this was the college that stated from the very beginning that men and women should always receive the same education, and that race should have no bearing, graduating the first black student in the 1880s. Dr. Arthur Holly Compton ('13) received the Nobel Prize in Physics in 1927, and Victor J. Andrew ('26) went on to create coaxial cable and the Andrew Corporation, which is used in every home in America today to broadcast television and satellite systems.

As of late, the College of Wooster has become more well-known to the rest of the world, and if you talk to someone who has heard of Wooster, their eyes widen and they nod vigorously, saying that they've heard stunning things about its reputation. And it's true. Again and again in the past few years the college has had praises rain down about its great curriculum, wonderful teachers, unique student body, excellent graduates, and so on and so forth.

But so what? Statistics may be nice and all, but what do the students think? And what does Wooster have to offer you? That, my friend, is why this book has been written. In the pages that follow, you will see both sides of every aspect of our college. You will come to understand why our graduates get misty looks on their faces at the shrill sound of the bagpipes. More importantly, you will understand the common bond among Wooster alumni and their relationships with each other, whether they graduated yesterday or 50 years ago. We may have great academics, dynamic professors, and national recognition, but above all, people who attend Wooster say it isn't just these things that matter, but the friends you meet along the way.

Sarah Core, Author
College of Wooster

By the Numbers

General Information

The College of Wooster
1189 Beall Avenue
Wooster, OH 44691

Control:
Private

Academic Calendar:
Semester

Religious Affiliation:
None

Founded:
1866

Web Site:
www.wooster.edu

Main Phone:
(330) 287-3000

Admissions Phone:
(800) 877-9905

Student Body

**Full-Time
Undergraduates:**
1,777

**Part-Time
Undergraduates:**
50

**Total Male
Undergraduates:**
854

**Total Female
Undergraduates:**
973

Admissions

Overall Acceptance Rate:
72%

Early Decision Acceptance Rate:
87%

Regular Acceptance Rate:
72%

Total Applicants:
2,523

Total Acceptances:
1,827

Freshman Enrollment:
488

Yield (percentage of admitted students who actually enroll):
27%

Early Decision Available?
Yes

Early Action Available?
No

Total Early Decision Applicants:
83

Total Early Decision Acceptances:
70

Early Decision One Deadline:
December 1

Early Decision Two Deadline:
January 15

Early Decision One Notification:
December 15

Early Decision Two Notification:
February 1

Regular Decision Deadline:
February 15

Regular Decision Notification:
April 1

Must-Reply-By Date:
May 1

Applicants Placed on Waiting List:
140

Applicants Accepted from Waiting List:
40

Students Enrolled from Waiting List:
34

Transfer Applications Received:
51

Transfer Applicants Accepted:
26

Transfer Students Enrolled:
12

Common Application Accepted?
Yes

Supplemental Forms?
Required

Admissions E-Mail:
admissions@wooster.edu

Admissions Web Site:
http://admissions.wooster.edu

SAT I or ACT Required?
Either

First-Year Students Submitting SAT Scores:
73%

SAT I Range (25th–75th Percentile):
1090–1330

SAT I Verbal Range (25th–75th Percentile):
540–670

SAT I Math Range (25th–75th Percentile):
550–660

Retention Rate:
87%

Top 10% of High School Class:
30%

Application Fee:
$40

Financial Information

Tuition:
$28,230

Room and Board:
$7,060

Books and Supplies:
$700

Average Need-Based Financial Aid Package (including loans, work-study, grants, and other sources):
$21,570

Students Who Applied for Financial Aid:
70%

Students Who Received Aid:
63%

Financial Aid Phone:
1-800-877-3688

Financial Aid E-Mail:
financialaid@wooster.edu

Financial Aid Web Site:
www.wooster.edu/financialaid

Academics

The Lowdown On...
Academics

Degrees Awarded:
Bachelor

Most Popular Majors:
9% History
9% Psychology
8% Communication Studies
8% Political Science
and Government
7% Sociology

Full-Time Faculty:
133

**Faculty with
Terminal Degree:**
97%

**Student-to-
Faculty Ratio:**
12:1

Average Class Size:
21

Average Course Load:
Four classes

Graduation Rates:
Four-Year: 63%
Five-Year: 68%
Six-Year: 68%

AP Test Score Requirements

Possible credit for scores of 3, 4, and 5

IB Test Score Requirements

Possible credit for scores of 3, 4, and 5

Special Degree Options

In conjunction with selected professional and graduate schools, the fourth year toward the BA degree is completed in the professional school.

Architecture (3-4 program with Washington University in Saint Louis)

Dentistry (3-4 program with Case Western Reserve University)

Engineering (3-4 program with Case Western Reserve, Michigan, and Washington University in Saint Louis)

Forestry & Environmental Studies (3-4 program with Duke University)

Nursing (3-4 program with Case Western Reserve University)

Social Work (3-4 program with Case Western Reserve University)

Best Places to Study

Dorm rooms and lounges, in the Lowry Student Center, and in the Timken and Gault Libraries

Did You Know?

The College of Wooster's **Independent Study (IS) program** was ranked the number two senior capstone experience in the nation, second only to Princeton University.

Wooster's **Student Volunteer Network**, which involves more than 400 of Wooster's 1,800 students in volunteer activities in the community, was recognized in 1991 by President George HW Bush as the 556th Daily Point of Light.

Wooster ranks **14th in the nation among independent colleges** whose male and female graduates earned PhDs between 1920 and 1995. (Baccalaureate Origins of Doctorate Recipients, 1998.)

People in Ohio pronounce things strangely! Wooster is actually pronounced "**Wu-ster**," and Beall and Bever Avenues, two of the main streets, have a funny tale that go along with them. They are pronounced "Bell" and "Beaver," and the old joke is that someone took the "a" out of Bever and put it in Beall, but forgot to change the pronunciation!

In the early '70s, **McGaw Chapel was supposed to be built underground**, but the contractors made a mistake. They didn't listen to the geology department, who told them they would hit bedrock! Sure enough, McGaw stands much taller than it was supposed to, but that's fine by students, who like to crawl up the sheer walls of its white towers and look out over the college campus late at night.

Students Speak Out On...
Academics

"Our professors rock! Make sure to pick classes that you are truly interested in, and never take a class because you hear that the professor is easy; you won't get anything out of those classes."

Q "The professors here at Woo are a ton of fun. All that I have had are interesting, absorbed in their subjects, and interested in me. I feel that they all know me, even though I may not speak individually with all of them. **Classes are always interesting**, especially the small ones!"

Q "There is an extremely broad range of professors on campus. There are some that are very personable and some that are just plain scary. Some are better teachers than others, and some are more professional in their student-teacher relationships. All in all, I think the **professors are generally very good**, very understanding, and kind. The classes vary on levels of interest mostly by what classes you choose to take. Required languages are not very fun (or interesting)."

Q "The professors are very keen on giving individual attention when needed. Students do not need to be shy when contacting professors personally. **Most classes are very engaging**, with the occasional very boring and uninteresting one."

Q "I think, in general, **the teachers are the best part** of this college."

Q "I would say that most of my teachers have been **very approachable and truly interested** in helping the students learn as much as they can."

Q "I think **the professors are caring, kind, approachable**, very knowledgeable, and usually very interesting."

Q "The professors are very down-to-earth and extremely qualified. **The most boring classes on earth** become awesome when you have the right teacher."

Q "Overall, I believe the professors here are terrific. In my major, I was able to form bonds that go beyond just teacher-student, and I am sure that I will be keeping in touch with them for years to come. Depending on the subject and your interest, **classes can be intriguing**. It is all a personal opinion."

Q "**The teachers can be really great**—really personally involved and interested not only in their subject, but in you, the student, too."

Q "My professors are really passionate and interested in what they're doing. **My classes are challenging and a lot of work**, but I'm also learning a lot, which will help me out in the real world."

Q "Most professors are excited about their particular field. It depends on the class as to whether or not it's exciting. **Classes with discussion are decidedly more interesting**."

Q "**The teachers at the College of Wooster are dynamic**, enthusiastic, and care deeply about each of their students' health and success."

The College Prowler Take On...
Academics

Students at Wooster regard academics in a serious way. From the classes to the professors, Wooster stands apart from the crowd because of its small class size, personal attention from professors, and individualized educational experience. Sure, you get that rare professor who drives you up the wall, but that isn't common at Wooster. Professors, not graduate or teaching assistants, teach all of the courses. Wooster also focuses on building good relationships between students and professors, and it encourages interaction through personal advising meetings and small class sizes. Classes at Wooster average 21 students, and never top 50. The professors all have office hours, and they are very willing to find time to meet with you after class, or respond to your e-mails. Some will even host special dinners at their houses, which is always a treat. The most boring subject can turn into an insightful and exciting foray on a subject you never knew about, as long as you have the right professor.

Wooster's curriculum stands as an example of its independent streak and school motto, "Scientia et Religio Ex Uno Fonte," which means "Knowledge and Religion from One Source." Students are exposed to a wide variety of subject matter, from intensive writing requirements to classes in traditional and non-traditional cultural thought and action. The pinnacle of a student's career at Wooster is the Senior Independent Study. For students, this is an opportunity to design a course in an area of study which particularly interests them. They can choose anything from writing a children's book for an English major to creating and performing a musical in front of the campus community.

The College Prowler® Grade on
Academics: A-

A high Academics grade generally indicates that professors are knowledgeable, accessible, and genuinely interested in their students' welfare. Other determining factors include class size, how well professors communicate, and whether or not classes are engaging.

Local Atmosphere

The Lowdown On...
Local Atmosphere

Region:
Midwest

City, State:
Wooster, Ohio

Setting:
Suburban

Distance from Washington DC:
6 hours, 30 minutes

Distance from Cleveland:
1 hour

Distance from Columbus:
2 hours

Distance from Pittsburgh:
2 hours, 30 minutes

Points of Interest:

Amish Country

Living Bible Museum

The J.M. Smucker Co. (Smucker's)

Wayne Center for the Arts

World's Largest Cuckoo Clock

Closest Shopping Mall or Plaza:

Lodi Outlets

9911 Avon Lake Rd. Unit 80 Burbank, Ohio 44214

(330) 948-9929

20 minutes north by car

Closest Movie Theaters:

The Big Picture

116 E South St., Wooster

(330) 263-6227

5 minutes south by car

Cinemark Movies 10

4108 Burbank Rd., Wooster

(330) 345-8816

5 minutes north by car

Major Sports Teams:

Cleveland Browns (football)

Cleveland Cavaliers (basketball)

Cleveland Indians (baseball)

City Web Sites

www.woostertoday.com

www.mainstreetwooster.org

www.wooster.net

Did You Know?

5 Fun Facts about Wooster:

- Wooster was the first place where **candy canes were hung on christmas trees**.
- The largest population of **Old Order Amish** lies just south of Wooster.
- The College sits on the **highest point of the city**.
- The **Ohio Light Opera** makes its summer home at the College.
- There is a large **corn maze** that runs through Ohio (visit *www.ramseyerfarms.com*).

Students Speak Out On...
Local Atmosphere

"The atmosphere in the town is weird. Sometimes, it feels like we are in the middle of nowhere. Correction—we are in the middle of nowhere!"

Q "Woo is a small Midwestern town. We've got a great Wally World, nice movie theater, some great restaurants, and some average ones. It is pretty much Anywhere, U.S.A. **I love it**!"

Q "**Wooster is a quaint little town**, and the sidewalks roll up around 6 p.m. Our Super Wal-Mart is the thing to do!"

Q "The community our college is in is a very close-knit one. There are a lot of churches in the area. There are also lots of Amish and Mennonites in the area, and it is interesting to see their way of life in comparison to my own. Ashland University and a branch of OSU are nearby. **Cleveland and Columbus are not too far away**."

Q "**The town is not very open to college students**. There are not any other colleges or universities. Definitely hit up Seattle's Coffee House downtown, Applebee's at 1 a.m., and CW's."

Q "The town of Wooster is the quintessential small Midwestern town. There's not a lot there, but enough to keep it from being entirely boring. **We're pretty much the only school for a ways**. The College seems to be a little bubble inside the city without really relating to it."

Q "It's quaint, in some places—very country-like, **a lot of churches**. However, downtown is pleasant and Wal-Mart is nearby, so you're never too far away from getting anything you need. Stay away from the townies, but go to Wal-Mart at least one Saturday night very, very late."

Q "Wooster is cute! There's not much to do in town except eat and watch movies. It's fun to look out your dorm room window and watch an Amish buggy go clip-clopping by. I find it hugely ironic that **there is a McDonald's right across the street** from a huge Catholic church. Some days, I almost expect the flashing digital sign to read, 'Fish Fry for Lent!'"

Q "**The town of Wooster is a classic, Midwestern town**, with wide streets and great historic buildings. There is a lot more to the town than meets the eye, so don't be fooled by just what you see. While there are other schools, our closest neighbor is Ohio State's agricultural school, so we don't hang out much. Be careful of the obnoxious townies."

Q "Wooster is a black hole. There is nothing to do. If it weren't for the campus, this place would be totally dead. The only other place is OSU/ATI, but **they dig in the dirt and feed cows**. Needless to say, they're not too interesting."

Q "The town is cute during the day. **They have little festivals**, and I love the restaurants. There isn't much to do at night besides the movie theater, but I always find something on campus, so I'm never bored. I know friends who go to the bars in town, but most aren't for college students. They are kind of sketchy."

Q "We don't really interact with the town very much, but **it's comfortable to go into town** to eat or shop. It seems that the town respects the college students. There are no other colleges or universities around. You should definitely visit the outlet mall. There really aren't any scary areas in town to stay away from. We're very safe."

Q "When describing where Wooster is, I always say in the middle of Amish country, but that is not necessarily true. Of course, the town is different from the College, but it can be interesting. **There isn't anywhere I'd stay away from**, but if you are like every college student, you'll definitely be spending time at Wal-Mart. Also, people like the corn mazes in the fall in Smithville, as well as the World's Largest Cuckoo Clock in Wilmot."

The College Prowler Take On...
Local Atmosphere

Let's face it, the city of Wooster is a small, quaint, Midwestern town in the heartland of Amish country. While it is said to be a great place to settle down and raise a family, the college scene is entirely different. Wooster is, needless to say, not a college town. The townspeople don't appreciate the college students on the weekends when they party off campus and park in their streets. The college kids don't appreciate the so-called 'townies' either, when they go blaring by in their cars, or when they shout out the windows at the girls walking down Beall Avenue, and especially when they give them tickets for parking their cars on the street.

However, there are many good things to be found in Wooster. While it may not be a bustling metropolis, there are certainly a lot of good interactions happening between the city and the College, especially in terms of volunteerism. About 400 students, which is almost a quarter of campus, are involved in the Wooster Volunteer Network, and they donate a lot of their time to helping out at the soup kitchen or tutoring children. Wooster is the county seat of Wayne County and has many events that college kids flock to, such as the county fair. There is also a great downtown with many quaint shops that students frequent during the day.

The College Prowler® Grade on

Local Atmosphere: C

A high Local Atmosphere grade indicates that the area surrounding campus is safe and scenic. Other factors include nearby attractions, proximity to other schools, and the town's attitude toward students.

Safety & Security

The Lowdown On...
Safety & Security

Number of Wooster Police:

8 full-time security officers
5 dispatchers
5 student supervisors
21 student patrol officers

Phone:

(330) 287-2590

Web Site:

www.wooster.edu/security

Wellness Center Office Hours:

Monday–Friday 8 a.m.–4 p.m.
(A registered nurse is staffed)
24 hours a day)

Safety Services:

Emergency blue-light phones
Engraver
Lockout service
Shuttle/escort van or personnel

➡

Health Services:

Basic medical services

On-site pharmaceuticals

Free ambulatory and 24-hour overnight care

Immunizations

STD screening

Did You Know?

The overnight rooms in the new Longbrake Student Wellness Center are equipped with cable television and Ethernet, and **your extension can even be transferred** to the room for the night!

Students Speak Out On...
Safety & Security

{ **"From what I've gathered so far, Wooster isn't as big on safety as they would like to promote the school to be when recruiting students or speaking with parents."**

Q "I think that Security and Safety are mainly doing their job, but I also think that **they sometimes exaggerate** on the alcohol issue."

Q "**Haha. Security**? If you need an escort, they usually send a five-foot boy who might pass as 15, but who would definitely not save you from anything save a few crazy squirrels. Otherwise, I think the campus is relatively safe. I wouldn't want to be walking around by myself really late at night, though. Then again, I wouldn't do that anywhere."

Q "The campus is fairly safe. **Occasionally, we have the stupid drunks,** and security can be very slow sometimes. Most of the time, though, there's nothing to worry about."

Q "**I've never had any trouble with them**. They are always available if you need a ride home to the dorm!"

Q "I personally do not feel very safe on campus. However, it is easy to travel in groups. If you're really desperate, you can get security to walk you to where you are going. I feel like **security does more of a job trying to get us in trouble** than actually protecting us."

Q "**Campus is pretty safe**, but there's always going to be a few incidents every year. Just be careful and in control of what you're doing, and you'll be fine."

Q "Safety and Security seem to always be around in the wrong places (parties) and absent when needed (vehicle break-ins). But **the guys are always friendly** and do help when needed."

Q "Security is pretty good, but I think **they could be more attentive** and present on campus, especially during the evening hours."

Q "When I was a freshman, Safety and Security was really bad, but over the past three years, they have been improving. **They still have a stigma attached to them**, but the student body is now better informed about the occasional issues on campus."

Q "I always feel secure on campus, although I do know there are occasional incidents. As with anywhere, **safety is in your hands**."

Q "Security is only a presence when they feel as though drinking may be occurring on campus or in a particular area. Other than that, **Security has never been much help to me**, and it was not a presence on campus when I needed them the most."

Q "**I feel pretty safe at Wooster**. I am from a small town myself, so Wooster doesn't make me nervous. There are a lot of little blue safety phones. However, now that I think about it, I really haven't seen too many adult security officers around."

Q "**I feel safe 99 percent of the time on campus**. If I don't feel safe, it's because of something stupid that I did. For instance, I found myself in a dark walkway alone at night."

The College Prowler Take On...
Safety & Security

Many students grow easily disgruntled with Safety and Security at Wooster. Security is normally seen as an enforcer of alcohol policies instead of a protector of the night. While they are watching out for the students' best interests and trying to protect them, students feel there is not much to keep them entertained. Certainly, serious security issues do come up, but compared to a big city, Wooster is the type of town where you could accidentally leave your garage door up all night and no one would steal a thing.

Safety and Security at Wooster remain very professional, offering the convenient services you would expect at a larger school. Since crime is rare, they work hard to make sure students are safe getting home on the weekends from whatever parties they may have attended. They are tough on underage students caught with a cup in their hands, though. This past year, security was completely revamped, and students say that the new security officers are personable, helpful, and just generally friendly.

B-

The College Prowler® Grade on

Safety & Security: B-

A high grade in Safety & Security means that students generally feel safe, campus police are visible, blue-light phones and escort services are readily available, and safety precautions are not overly necessary.

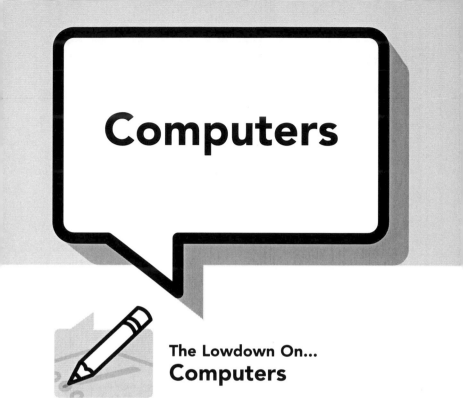

Computers

The Lowdown On...
Computers

High-Speed Network?
T3 connection

Wireless Network?
Available in Lowry Student Center, libraries, and various academic buildings

Number of Labs:
3 public labs
5 partial labs
6 academic labs
1 cyber café

Numbers of Computers:
500

Operating Systems:
Mac OS 9
ME
OS X
Windows 05
Windows NT
XP Professional

Free Software

Eudora, Macromedia Dreamweaver, Maple, McAfee, Novell, and VirusScan

Discounted Software

Adobe Acrobat, Keyserve (free access on campus), Microsoft Office Software Package, and Microsoft XP Professional and Standard

24-Hour Labs

Cyber cafè

Charge to Print?

Each student at the College is provided with a certain amount of paper each year. Freshmen and sophomores get 1,200 pages, juniors receive 1,500, and seniors get 1,800 pages. After you reach your limit, each page is $.05 a copy.

Did You Know?

Each Wooster student receives a **Permanent Personal Extension (PPX)** in the summer before their first year. That four-digit extension will remain with the student no matter where he or she lives on the campus. The PPX may be dialed direct from one campus extension to another. Off-campus callers dial (330) 287-3000, and enter either the student's PPX or follow instructions to dial by name. Every PPX includes voicemail at no charge.

Students Speak Out On...
Computers

> "We no longer have computer labs in the dorms, and having your own computer is very common. I have a laptop, and I love it, because I can bring it to the library or to the Wired Scot, our new cyber café."

Q "**I have my own computer**. It is just more convenient that way, since the computer labs close at one and 2 a.m. I've never seen a lab too crowded to hold all the students who want to use them."

Q "The network is free to students, but it tends to go down sometimes. **Computer labs are never crowded**, and most students have their own computers. I like to use the computer labs to write papers, because my dorm room is too noisy."

Q "Computer labs are usually available. **The Internet is still pretty slow**. I would recommend bringing your own computer."

Q "Definitely bring your own computer. The network is fine and **seems really fast** if you're used to a dial up connection, but the facilities for computers are somewhat out of the way, depending on your living situation."

Q "**I've never really had a problem with computers**—but I have my own. The library always has some available, and they are well maintained."

Q "Our computer network is generally okay, but **our college lacks computer labs** for the underprivileged students. A cyber café does not make up for this loss."

Q "Computer labs are always crowded, and the printers never work. Bring your own computer and printer. **The labs are there if you need them**, but a personal computer is a really nice addition to life."

Q "**Bring your own computer** unless you want to hike back and forth to the labs every day. Trust me, five minutes is really long when it's snowing!"

Q "Printing was temporarily a problem this year, but normally, there are no problems on the network. I think **every student should have their own computer** if possible!"

Q "I highly recommend bringing your own computer. **They just removed the computer labs from the dorms**. Although they created one in the main campus building, it won't be fun to walk to late at night."

Q "**The network is generally reliable**. I really don't use computer labs, but, when I walk past, they don't seem too crowded. I would bring your own computer. It is so much more convenient. Plus, AIM is a way of life around here."

Q "Buy a laptop. It saves space and is portable. The computer people try their best to help if you have a problem. **There is rarely a wait for computers** in the labs."

Q "**I strongly recommend that students have their own laptop** and printer, preferably one with a built in scanner for photo-copying and scanning pictures."

Q "Definitely bring your own computer. There will be computers to use, but it's that much easier if you have your own. However, **it doesn't matter if you bring a Mac or PC**, because the network supports both kinds."

Q "Well, considering **there are no more computer labs in the dorms anymore**, it can be kind of a hassle. I think there are enough computers for people without one. I think you might as well save your money and not buy a computer if you have to walk all the way to the library to print a paper out, because you might as well just work on it there."

Q "**Computer labs are not usually crowded** at all because most students bring computers. I would suggest bringing one because it makes life easier, but you certainly don't need to."

Q "The computer network is simply an Ethernet connection available for PCs or Macs. **The computer labs are not crowded often** (except for IS time), but the idea of having your own computer is beneficial. Frankly, when it comes to walking in the snow to a computer, I would rather be in my room instead."

The College Prowler Take On...
Computers

Personal computers are essential to surviving at Wooster. However, the existing computer faculties are not as good as they could be. Recently, IT made the decision to remove all computer labs from the dorms, because the labs were not being efficiently used, and they felt that they needed more room for students to live. While most students do have their own computers, some things, like printing online reading assignments, are done much more efficiently on the school's computers. Printers also used to be located in each dorm. The absence of these printers means that students without printers now need to walk to one of three computer labs around campus to print their papers.

Computer labs are situated in the libraries and the computer center, and are available for student's use until one and 2 a.m. on the weeknights. The new cyber café is located in the basement of Lowry Student Center and is open 24 hours. However, it is set up as a place for students to check their e-mail and grab a cup of coffee, as well as print out their papers, not necessarily for late-night studying.

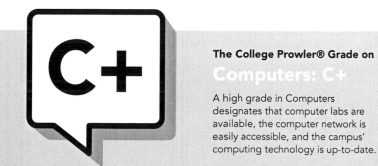

C+

The College Prowler® Grade on
Computers: C+

A high grade in Computers designates that computer labs are available, the computer network is easily accessible, and the campus' computing technology is up-to-date.

Facilities

The Lowdown On...
Facilities

Student Center:
Lowry Student Center

Athletic Center:
The Armington Physical
Education Center

Libraries:
3

Campus Size:
240 acres

→

Popular Places to Chill:

Common Grounds – A student-run program house, the main floor has been designed as a coffeehouse where students can come and hang out with friends and listen to live music.

The Quad – When summer comes, students flock to any available green space to nap in the sun, play a game of Frisbee, read a book, or even create a following by playing the guitar!

Scot Lanes – In the basement of Lowry Student Center is a bowling alley, complete with Ping-Pong, arcade games, a jukebox, pool tables, and a large screen TV. Students love to go hang out with their friends there. Cosmic Bowling is a favorite activity.

The Shack – South of campus near the Admissions building, the Shack is a great place to grab breakfast or sit and relax.

What Is There to Do on Campus?

WAC, the Wooster Activities Crew, is very vocal. They are constantly providing entertainment, both on and off campus, to students at Wooster. In one day, you could go bowling and play pool right after classes, have high tea at 4 p.m., watch a drive-in movie later in the evening on the football field, and then go dancing at the Underground into the wee hours of the morning.

Movie Theater on Campus?

The Film Club shows movies once a week in Luce Hall and WAC also provides on- and off-campus cheap movie tickets and showings.

Bowling on Campus?

Yes, Scot Lanes in the basement of Lowry Student Center.

Bar on Campus?

Yes, the College Underground

Coffeehouse on Campus?

Yes, Common Grounds and the Java Hut

Favorite Things to Do

Wooster holds forums all the time, and many students go to see those, because not only are they usually educational, but Wooster has been able to procure some intriguing people, such as Michael Moore. Scot Lanes is always a fun place to hang out, as is the Quad on a sunny day. Students rarely find themselves bored, though, because often one organization or another is hosting a blood drive, or a theme week, which involves food, crafts, dancing, or even something like a dog-petting day.

Students Speak Out On...
Facilities

"Wooster's facilities are good. I can't complain about any of the buildings. Our new psychology and economics building, Morgan Hall, is beautiful. I love it."

Q "Our facilities are nice, and are getting better! We have **tons of new computers in Lowry**."

Q "The facilities are well maintained, but I wish they would turn the lights off more. It's a ridiculous waste of energy. My favorite building on campus, I would have to say is—I can't choose! **Timken Library is the place to be**, Wagner Hall is awesome, and Kenarden Lounge is really great."

Q "Honestly, **I feel that for the price of our tuition**, things should and could be better on this tiny, rural campus. Some of the dorms are badly in need of an upgrade."

Q "**I am a huge fan of the science library**, which was built over 100 years ago, but is utterly gorgeous and very modern, too. It's my favorite place to study."

Q "**My favorite building is Kauke Hall** because I spend my life there—both my major and minor are there. It needs to be renovated. It's still great that we have buildings that are over 100 years old, because it really adds to the beauty and atmosphere of the campus. The science library is awesome—I wish I was a science major! Even our dorms are architecturally gorgeous. I love living in them, because they have a real college feel to them."

Q "**The facilities are usually pretty nice**, but some places look like they have furniture from over 30 years ago."

Q "**Lowry leaves a lot to be desired**. For that matter, so does the PEC. The Wired Scot is about the only thing that looks half-decent around here. All of the public spaces need a major overhaul. Morgan is nice, but Kauke is awful! Thankfully, it will soon be renovated."

Q "The majority of the buildings are really nice, and efforts are continuously being made to improve and redo them. They aren't ostentatious, but **they're elegant**."

Q "Overall, facilities are okay. I admit that many things need to be renovated so they are more up-to-date, but they **get the job done**. Severance Hall and the science library are gorgeous, but Lowry could definitely use some more appeal since it is the student center. The PEC is also a little small, but they are going to be upgrading that soon, we hope."

The College Prowler Take On...
Facilities

Wooster is old and lovingly maintained. The grass is clipped, the flowers are bright, and the beautiful old stonework on the buildings glistens in the sun (on the good days). The majority of the academic buildings have been restored in the past 10 years, which makes for great working facilities. The student end of campus, though, is a different story. That isn't to say that they aren't great buildings. It's just getting to be a tight fit. Students are crammed into dorms and small houses, crammed into the student center, and packed into the Physical Education Center as well.

However, the College has done an honorable job of keeping up with everything, and they are aware of what still needs to be done. Recently the students received a brand new Wellness Center, which is in top technological form, as well as a new admissions center. The winter of 2001-02, one million dollars was invested into revamping Lowry, the main dining hall on campus, as a winter surprise. In the fall of 2002, a new academic building was opened to the campus for use, and everyone in academics breathed a little easier. The 12th dorm on campus, Bornhuetter Hall, has just been completed and provides students with more breathing room.

B

The College Prowler® Grade on

Facilities: B

A high Facilities grade indicates that the campus is aesthetically pleasing and well-maintained; facilities are state-of-the-art, and libraries are exceptional. Other determining factors include the quality of both athletic and student centers and an abundance of things to do on campus.

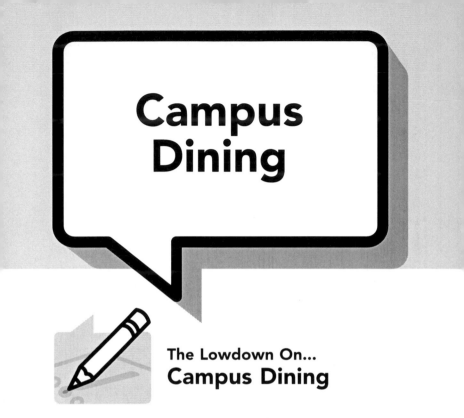

Campus Dining

The Lowdown On...
Campus Dining

Freshman Meal Plan Requirement?

Yes

Meal Plan Average Cost:

$1,075 per semester

Places to Grab a Bite with Your Meal Plan:

The Java Hut

Food: Features grab-n-go breakfasts and lunches, with bagels, coffee, and sweet items in the mornings, and pre-made deli style options for lunch. Also has Starbucks available.

Location: Lowry Student Center, basement

Hours: Monday–Friday 7 a.m.–1 p.m., Saturday–Sunday 7 a.m.–11 a.m.

→

Kittredge Dining Hall

Food: A certified "No-Fry Zone," Kittredge has a more home-style feel to its cooking and provides healthier options. Kittredge also houses the "Soup & Bread" charity group.

Location: Kittredge Hall, attached to Compton Hall

Hours: Monday–Friday 11 a.m.–1:30 p.m., 5 p.m.–7 p.m.

Lowry Center Dining Hall

Food: Lowry features cooked-to-order food stations, an International station, fruit and salad bars, a grill station, fresh-oven pizza, a deli, a pasta line, a meat and potatoes line, Edy's ice cream, and fresh-out-of-the-oven cookies.

Location: Lowry Student Center

Hours: Monday–Saturday 7:30 a.m.–8 p.m., Sunday 10:30 a.m.–8 p.m.

Mom's Truck Stop & Woo Mart

Food: Grill style, simple fast food options that are a little heartier. It's a great place to come late at night to get a snack and quiet enough to study.

Location: Lowry Student Center, basement

Hours: Sunday–Saturday 11 a.m–12 a.m., (Grill open 11 a.m.–3 p.m., and 5 p.m.–11:30 p.m.)

The Wooster Inn

Food: Fine dining, hot entrees, wines and other drink specialties, desserts, and several grilled items

Location: Central Campus

Hours: Tuesday–Thursday 7 a.m.–2 p.m., 4:30 p.m.–8 p.m., Friday–Saturday 7 a.m.–2 p.m., 4:30 p.m.–9 p.m., Sunday 11 a.m.–2 p.m.

Off-Campus Places to Use Your Meal Plan:
None

24-Hour On-Campus Eating?
No, only vending machines

Student Favorites:
The Java Hut
Kittredge Dining Hall
Mom's Truck Stop & Woo Mart

Students Speak Out On...
Campus Dining

> "Both dining halls serve excellent food. I'm a vegetarian (who is slowly going vegan), and I have yet to get sick of the food here at Wooster. I'd recommend Lowry's international food line."

Q "Overall, the food is decent. Eating at Lowry strengthens your culinary creativity. Kittredge is always **good for a home-style meal**."

Q "**The food is decent**. It's sometimes repetitive, though. Grab-n-go lunches are the best thing that happened to Lowry since they added an extra worker in the grill station."

Q "This is the one thing I have found to be horrible at Wooster. While Kittredge has far better food than Lowry, it does not have much variety. **Lowry serves food soaked in grease**."

Q "**I love the food at Wooster**. Others may disagree, but I think, especially for dining halls, there is a good variety. It's well prepared, and for growing boys like me, there's a lot to eat!"

Q "Our food is great, especially at Kittredge. **There are definitely a lot of choices**."

Q "The food is cafeteria food. I am a vegetarian, and the selection tends to get a bit slim at times, but I always survive. Take Tupperware, and **plan on stealing fruit and cereal**."

Q "Kittredge has your mom's home-cooking feel to it, while Lowry is more like the food court at the mall. The food is pretty good; you just have to be careful how you eat or else **you will gain a lot of weight**."

Q "**The dining halls are pretty nice**, but it's the usual problem that familiarity breeds contempt, and by the end of the year, everyone is sick of it all."

Q "The food is okay but can be repetitive. **Mom's is a great place to snack late at night**—the fries there are great. Kittredge is the best dining hall. It's relaxing and warm."

Q "The Food Services work really hard to make great meals for us. Even though **the food can get repetitive**, it's still awesome compared to anywhere else. What other college feeds you sushi, cous cous, and omelets every day? Where else takes an entire dining hall outside for a barbeque with 1,000 students?"

Q "**I like the food**. It is really good for being cafeteria food. Kittredge Dining Hall is great. Go there."

Q "The food here keeps me from undertaking **periodic hunger strikes**."

Q "The food is fine. Some things are wonderful, and **some things suck**. If you're adventurous enough, you can go weeks without eating the same thing twice."

Q "**I like the food here at Wooster**. I actually crave it over the summer. Both Kittredge and Lowry, if you can believe it. I know it lacks in change as the year goes on, but there is a lot of variety in general. At home, I'm always left scrounging in the fridge for frozen things; at Wooster, I get pampered."

Q "I think **the food on campus is very diverse**, and it's definitely better than at my friends' schools. I mean, guys love our dining hall—it's all you can eat!"

Q "The food is pretty good, but **sometimes the variety suffers**. The dining halls are really nice."

Q "Food is pretty good on campus. As with any campus, you will get tired of it after a while. **The people who work in the cafeterias are always friendly**. I have gotten to know some of them really well, and I occasionally chat to them for a while."

The College Prowler Take On...
Campus Dining

Campus dining is a mixed bag of tricks. The College keeps tweaking with the meal plan, and every year, Wooster takes baby steps in the right direction. The big improvement is the ability to swipe your meal card any three times a day you please, and the new grab-n-go lunches downstairs in Lowry Student Center. However, students still would like to be able to use their meal card in Mom's Truck Stop and the Shack down the road.

Overall, the College seems to have a very good system. The all-you-can-eat buffet style is one not seen often at colleges and universities anymore, and Wooster's repertoire of food is rather varied. Visitors from other colleges in the area rate it very high when they eat with us. Although it can grow repetitive, students like that they know who is cooking what they eat. They are also appreciative of the ID card swipe ladies that call them by name. It's the small touches that make eating more enjoyable.

The College Prowler® Grade on

Campus Dining: B

Our grade on Campus Dining addresses the quality of both school-owned dining halls and independent on-campus restaurants as well as the price, availability, and variety of food.

Off-Campus Dining

The Lowdown On...
Off-Campus Dining

Restaurant Prowler:
Popular Places to Eat!

The Amish Door
Food: Amish, American
6655 Lincoln Way E (U.S. 30)
(330) 263-0547
Cool Features: Family-style offered, great Sunday brunch bar in a real converted barn.
Price: $20 and under per person
Hours: Monday–Saturday 7 a.m.–8 p.m.

El Canelo
Food: Mexican
4782 Cleveland Rd.
(330) 345-7005
Cool Features: Fast service, steaming hot authentic food with complimentary nachos.
Price: $10 and under per person
Hours: Monday–Thursday 11 a.m.–10 p.m., Friday–Saturday 11 a.m.–11 p.m., Sunday 11 a.m.–9 p.m.

Coccia House Ristorante & Pizzeria

Food: Italian, American

764 Pittsburgh Ave.

(330) 262-7136

Cool Features: Everything here is homemade, legendary pizza and a full service bar.

Price: $25 and under per person

Hours: Sunday–Thursday 5 p.m.–11 p.m.., Friday– Saturday 5 p.m.–12 a.m., (closed Tuesdays)

Country Kitchen

Food: American

2179 Lincoln Way E (U.S. 30)

(330) 262-4106

Cool Features: Go whenever you have a large group of hungry and cheap people.

Price: $10 and under per person

Hours: Open 24 hours

CW Burgerstein's Great Sandwich Works

Food: American

359 W Liberty St.

(330) 264-6263

Cool Features: The best wings in town, gourmet burgers, a wide selection of specialty sandwiches and drinks.

Price: $15 and under per person

Hours: Monday–Thursday 11 a.m.–9:30 p.m., Friday– Saturday 11 a.m.–12 a.m.

El Campesino

Food: Mexican

177 Milltown Rd.

(330) 345-6263

Cool Features: Great Mexican food served quickly with authentic margaritas.

Price: $15 and under per person

Hours: Monday–Thursday 11 a.m.–10 p.m., Friday 11 a.m.–10:30 p.m., Saturday 12 p.m.–10:30 p.m, Sunday 11:30 a.m.–9 p.m.

Fazoli's Restaurant

Food: Italian, American

4142 Burbank Rd.

(330) 345-1923

Cool Features: Fast-food Italian! Speedy and utterly delicious!

Price: $10 and under per person

Hours: Monday–Friday 10:30 a.m.–9:30 p.m., Saturday 4:30 p.m.–9:30 p.m.

Hop Hing Chinese Restaurant

Food: Chinese

1805 Beall Ave.

(330) 263-4500

Cool Features: Lots of fast Chinese food.

Price: $10 and under per person

Hours: Monday–Thursday 11 a.m.–10 p.m., Friday– Saturday 11 a.m.–10:30 p.m., Sunday 12 p.m.–10 p.m.

→

K-D Pizza & Subs

Food: Pizza

602 E Bowman

(330) 264-7144

Cool Features: Free delivery, one medium, one topping is $5.95, and they have a great subs, spuds, and soda offer.

Price: $5 and under per person

Hours: Sunday–Thursday 11 a.m.–1 a.m., Friday 11 a.m.–2 a.m., Saturday 3 p.m.–2 a.m.

Matsos' Family Restaurant & Pizza

Food: Greek

154 W Liberty St.

(330) 264-8800

Cool Features: Homemade Greek dressing for sale!

Price: $13 and under per person

Hours: Tuesday–Thursday 11 a.m.–9 p.m., Friday–Saturday 11 a.m.–8 p.m., Sunday 11:30 a.m.–9 p.m.

The Olde Jaol Brewing Company

Food: American

215 N Walnut St.

(330) 262-3333

Cool Features: Indoor and outdoor options, a full tavern, converted from a real jail where you can dine in "cells" with a classy menu.

Price: $40 and under per person

(The Olde Jaol Brewing Company, continued)

Hours: Monday–Saturday 4:30 p.m.–10 p.m.

Primo's Deli

Food: American

3860 Cleveland Rd.

(330) 345-1314

Cool Features: A great deli and small restaurant, to-die-for desserts, and they deliver.

Price: $15 and under per person

Hours: Monday–Saturday 11 a.m.–9 p.m., Sunday 11 a.m.–8 p.m.

The Shack

Food: Breakfast, American

437 E Pine St.

(330) 262-9665

Cool Features: The traditional Wooster hangout for over 50 years.

Price: $15 and under per person

Hours: Monday–Thursday 7 a.m.–3 p.m., Friday–Saturday 7 a.m.–8 p.m., Sunday 7 a.m.–5 p.m.

South Market Bistro

Food: French-American

151 S Market St.

(330) 264-3663

Cool Features: Creative, healthy dining with a casual, French feel.

→

(South Market Bistro, continued)

Price: $30 and under per person

Hours: Monday–Thursday 11 a.m.–2 p.m., 5:30 p.m.–9:30 p.m., Friday–Saturday 5 p.m.–10:30 p.m.

TJ's Restaurant & Catering

Food: American

359 W Liberty St.

(330) 264-6263

Cool Features: Features prime ribs, steak, fresh seafood, private rooms, and cocktails.

Price: $30 and under per person

Hours: Monday–Friday 11 a.m.–9:30 p.m., Saturday 4:30 p.m.–9:30 p.m.

Wild Ginger China Bistro

Food: Chinese

3694 Burbank Rd.

(330) 345-6388

Cool Features: High-class Chinese dining with modern feel and fresh food daily from Cleveland.

Price: $25 and under per person

Hours: Sunday–Thursday 11 a.m.–9 p.m., Friday–Saturday 11 a.m.–10 p.m.

Student Favorites:

El Canelo

CW Burgerstein's Great Sandwich Works

South Market Bistro

24-Hour Eating:

Country Kitchen

→

Other Places to Check Out:

Applebee's (American)

Buehler's Mill Restaurant (American)

Buffalo Wild Wings

Hong Kong Buffet (Chinese)

Longhorn Steakhouse (Steak)

The Mill

Muddy Waters Café (Variety)

Papa John's (Pizza)

Red Lobster (Seafood)

Tumbleweed

Wooster Inn

Closest Grocery Stores:

Buehler's
3540 Burbank Rd.
Wooster, OH 44691
(330) 345-5908

Drug Mart
625 Beall Ave.
Wooster, OH 44691
(330) 264-8404

Wal-Mart
3883 Burbank Rd.
Wooster, OH 44691
(330) 345-8955

Wooster Food Co-Op
138 E Liberty St.
Wooster, OH 44691
(330) 264-9797

Late-Night, Half-Price Food Specials:

McDonald's (Free apple pies near closing time—midnight.)

Best Breakfast:

The Shack

Best Wings:

CW Burgerstein's Great Sandwich Works

Best Healthy:

South Market Bistro

Best Pizza:

K-D Pizza & Subs

Best Chinese:

Hop Hing Chinese Restaurant

Best Place to Take Your Parents:

The Olde Jaol Brewing Company

TJ's Restaurant & Catering

Students Speak Out On...
Off-Campus Dining

"I'm big on healthy food, so I love the Wooster Co-Op store downtown, as well as South Market Bistro, which also has amazing food."

Q "**There are plenty of great restaurants**. The pizza places all offer a $5.95 college special! There's always Papa John's."

Q "My girlfriend and I love to go to Matsos', which is **very classy and grown-up**, yet it has nice prices."

Q "There are fast food chains everywhere, and we have snazzier places like Longhorn Steakhouse and Red Lobster as well. **Check out Fazoli's**! It's a killer Italian fast food joint with cheap prices."

Q "There is a really nice French restaurant in the square downtown, but **it's kind of expensive**, as is the Wooster Inn. There's also a lot of fast food for a quick, cheap meal."

Q "Unfortunately, Wooster is not a huge town, so there are not a ton of restaurants. Matsos' is an awesome Greek place, mainly because of the owner Spiro and his fantastic food and attitude. My parents always love the Mill at Buehler's because it is home cooking. **The Olde Jaol is a lot of fun**."

Q "I love Chinese food, and there is a lot of it in Wooster. **My favorite places are Hop Hing (a family-owned takeout place)**, Hong Kong buffet (filling and cheap), and the Wild Ginger (an upscale place with the most fabulous food on the planet)."

Q "There are a lot of restaurants off campus. CW Burgerstein's (bar and grill) and the Olde Jaol are two downtown favorites. Also, there are **a lot of chains** such as Applebee's, Tumbleweed, and many others."

Q "The Olde Jaol has really exemplary, amazing food, but it's a little pricey. **CW's has great wings on Wednesday nights for really cheap**. South Market is also good if your parents are willing to pay."

Q "**There are tons of really fun, homey restaurants** off campus. Amish restaurants are everywhere, and places like the Amish Door are the best."

Q "El Canelo and El Campesino are really great Mexican places in town. El Canelo has the better and cheaper food, but **El Campesino serves great mixed drinks**."

Q "**The restaurants are delicious**. My favorites include CW's and Primo's Deli."

Q "**The restaurants off campus are decent**, and some are great. South Market Bistro, TJ's, Coccia House, El Canelo, and Muddy Waters Café are a few of the best."

Q "I am always going off campus to eat because **there are tons of great places**. Check out CW's, the Olde Jaol Tavern, and El Canelo."

Q "I love Wild Ginger. It's nice and classy and cheap. For the amount of food you get, it's ridiculously cheap. For the size of the town we are in, **Wooster has the restaurant scene covered**."

Q "I just went to the South Market Bistro last weekend, and it was the some of the best food ever. **I want to go back right now**."

The College Prowler Take On...
Off-Campus Dining

While the city of Wooster may not have many attractions, they know how to eat, and eat well here in Ohio. If the dining hall food is getting to you, there are plenty of great places off campus to enjoy a fabulous meal at nice prices. Most of the restaurants in the area are classy yet still reasonably priced. Those places that are not inexpensive, however, are well worth the money spent to get fantastic food.

The restaurant selection has steadily improved over the last 10 years. While made up of both family-owned restaurants and smaller chains, expansion in the area has also seen several popular chains, such as Buffalo Wild Wings, move in. A local favorite is Matsos', a family-owned authentic Greek restaurant located in downtown Wooster. Local pizza places are very kind to the college community. Most offer student discounts which drop the price for a large one-topper to a rock bottom $6. There has also been an upsurge in places that deliver, making it possible to enjoy high-quality food without leaving campus.

B+

The College Prowler® Grade on

Off-Campus Dining: B+

A high Off-Campus Dining grade implies that off-campus restaurants are affordable, accessible, and worth visiting. Other factors include the variety of cuisine and the availability of alternative options (vegetarian, vegan, Kosher, etc.).

Campus Housing

The Lowdown On...
Campus Housing

Room Types:
Singles, doubles, triples

Best Dorms:
Andrews
Douglass
Kenarden

Worst Dorms:
Bissman
Holden Annex

Undergrads Living on Campus:
99%

Number of Dormitories:
12 (32 program houses)

Number of University-Owned Apartments:
0

→

Dormitories:

Andrews Hall

Floors: 3 + basement

Total Occupancy: 76

Bathrooms: 6, Shared by floor or section

Coed: Yes, by floor

Residents: Freshmen

Room Types: Doubles and triples

Program: First-Year Experience

Special Features: Laundry facilities; vending machines; a kitchen area with a stove, refrigerator, and microwave; a bicycle room; a TV lounge; a large multipurpose room

Armington Hall

Floors: 4 + basement

Total Occupancy: 145

Bathrooms: 10, Shared by floor or section

Coed: Yes, by section

Residents: Seniors

Room Types: Singles and doubles

Program: Senior Experience

Special Features: Laundry facilities; vending machines; a kitchen area with a stove, refrigerator, microwave, and table; a bicycle room; formal and informal lounges

Babcock Hall

Floors: 3 + basement

Total Occupancy: 114

(Babcock Hall, continued)

Bathrooms: 7, shared by floor or section

Coed: Yes, by section

Residents: International students (all classes)

Room Types: Singles, doubles, and triples

Program: International

Special Features: Laundry facilities; vending machines; a kitchen area with a stove, refrigerator, and microwave; a bicycle room; a TV lounge and rec. room; large formal lounge; dining/study room; two small lounges

Bissman Hall

Floors: 4 + basement

Total Occupancy: 137

Bathrooms: 10, shared by floor or section

Coed: Yes, by section

Residents: All classes

Room Types: Singles and doubles

Program: Clubs and Sections

Special Features: Laundry facilities; vending machines; a kitchen area with a stove, refrigerator, microwave, and table; a bicycle room; formal and informal lounges

Bomhuetter Hall

Floors: 3 + basement

Total Occupancy: 185

Bathrooms: 8, shared by floor

Coed: Yes, by floor

(Bomhuetter Hall, continued)

Residents: All classes

Room Types: Doubles

Special Features: Laundry facilities; vending machines; a kitchen area with a stove, refrigerator, microwave, and table; a bicycle room; formal and informal lounges

Compton Hall

Floors: 3 + basement

Total Occupancy: 115

Bathrooms: 8, shared by floor or section

Coed: No, all females

Residents: All classes

Room Types: Singles and doubles

Special Features: Laundry facilities; vending machines; a kitchen area with a stove, refrigerator, microwave, and table; a bicycle room; a formal lounge; two large multi-purpose rooms

Douglass Hall

Floors: 3 + basement

Total Occupancy: 116

Bathrooms: 7, Shared by floor

Coed: Yes, by floor

Residents: All classes

Room Types: Singles, doubles, and triples

(Douglass Hall, continued)

Special Features: Laundry facilities; vending machines; a kitchen area with a stove, refrigerator, microwave, and table; a bicycle room; a formal lounge; a TV lounge; a large multipurpose room

Holden Hall

Floors: 3 + basement

Total Occupancy: 262

Bathrooms: 12, shared by floor or section

Coed: Yes, by floor or section

Residents: All classes

Room Types: Singles, doubles, and triples

Special Features: Laundry facilities; vending machines; a kitchen area with a stove, refrigerator, microwave, and table; a bicycle room; two formal lounges; TV lounge; study lounge

Holden Annex

Floors: 2

Total Occupancy: 48

Bathrooms: 2, shared by floor

Coed: Yes, by floor

Residents: All classes

Room Types: Doubles

Special Features: Laundry facilities, an informal lounge, television room

Kenarden Lodge

Floors: 3 + basement

Total Occupancy: 141

Bathrooms: 10, shared by floor or section

Coed: Yes, by floor or section

Residents: All classes

Room Types: Singles, doubles, triples, and suite triples

Special Features: Laundry facilities; vending machines; a kitchen area with a stove, refrigerator, microwave, and table; convenience areas with sinks and microwaves; a bicycle room; a formal lounge with a spiral staircase; TV lounge; fitness room

Luce Hall

Floors: 3 + basement

Total Occupancy: 98

Bathrooms: 18, shared by section or suite

Coed: Yes, by floor or hall

Residents: Upperclassmen

Room Types: Singles and doubles

Program: Language Suites

Special Features: Laundry facilities; vending machines; a kitchen area with a stove, refrigerator, microwave, and table; convenience areas with sinks and microwaves; a bicycle room; a TV lounge; a large formal lounge; multipurpose room with projection TV; language laboratory; fitness room

Stevenson Hall

Floors: 4 + basement

Total Occupancy: 88

Bathrooms: 7, shared by floor or section

Coed: Yes, by section

Residents: Seniors

Room Types: Singles

Program: Senior Experience

Special Features: Laundry facilities; vending machines; a kitchen area with a stove, microwave, and table; TV lounge; formal lounge

Wagner Hall

Floors: 3 + basement

Total Occupancy: 122

Bathrooms: 5, shared by floor or section

Coed: Yes, by floor or section

Residents: Freshmen

Room Types: Singles and doubles

Program: First-Year Experience

Special Features: Laundry facilities; vending machines; a kitchen area with a stove, refrigerator, microwave, and table; informal lounge; formal lounge; TV lounge

Program Houses:

At Wooster, program houses are a large part of the campus community. The Wooster Volunteer Network involves over 400 students on campus in volunteer program living and for students who share a common interest. These programs should include a service aspect, such as volunteering for a local agency, or may be designed to offer programs that will educate the community about a specific topic or interest.

Aultz House

Floors: 2 + basement

Total Occupancy: 7

Bathrooms: 2

Room Types: Singles and doubles

Program: German

Special Features: Laundry facilities; a kitchen area with a stove, refrigerator, table and chairs, and a living room

Avery House

Floors: 2 + basement

Total Occupancy: 7

Bathrooms: 2

Room Types: Singles and doubles

Program: French

Special Features: Laundry facilities; a kitchen area with a stove, refrigerator, table and chairs, and a living room

Bontrager House

Floors: 2 + basement

Total Occupancy: 10

Bathrooms: 2

Room Types: Doubles

Program: Sunrise Assisted Living

Special Features: Laundry facilities; a kitchen area with a stove, refrigerator, table and chairs, a living room, and dining room

Bryan House

Floors: 2 + basement

Total Occupancy: 11

Bathrooms: 2

Room Types: Singles and doubles

Program: Ohio READs

Special Features: Laundry facilities; a kitchen area with a stove, refrigerator, table and chairs, a living room, and dining room

Calcei House

Floors: 2 + basement

Total Occupancy: 8

Bathrooms: 2

Room Types: Singles and doubles

Program: Chinese

Special Features: Laundry facilities; a kitchen area with a stove, refrigerator, table and chairs, a living room

Colonial House

Floors: 3 + basement

Total Occupancy: 10

Room Types: Singles and doubles

Program: Women of Images

Special Features: Laundry facilities; a kitchen area with a stove, refrigerator, table and chairs, a living room, and dining room

Corner House

Floors: 3 + basement

Total Occupancy: 12

Room Types: Singles and doubles

Program: The Gallows

Special Features: Laundry facilities; a kitchen area with a stove, refrigerator, table and chairs, a living room, and dining room

Crandall Apartments

Floors: 2 + basement

Total Occupancy: 6

Room Types: Doubles

Program: Organic Farming

Special Features: Laundry facilities; a kitchen area with a stove, refrigerator, table and chairs, a living room

Gable House

Floors: 2 + basement

Total Occupancy: 9

(Gable House, continued)

Room Types: Singles and doubles

Program: Common Grounds

Special Features: Laundry facilities; a kitchen area with a stove, refrigerator, microwave, table and chairs, a living room, a front parlor, a back rec. room.

Grosjean House

Floors: 3 + basement

Total Occupancy: 7

Room Types: Singles and doubles

Program: French

Special Features: Laundry facilities; a kitchen area with a stove, refrigerator, table and chairs, a living room, and dining room

Hider Apartments

Floors: 1 + basement, 2 sections

Total Occupancy: 10

Room Types: Doubles

Program: Organic Farming

Special Features: Laundry facilities; a kitchen area with a stove, refrigerator, table and chairs in each section, a living room in each section

Hider House

Floors: 3 + basement

Total Occupancy: 9

Room Types: Singles and doubles

(Hider House, continued)

Program: German

Special Features: Laundry facilities; a kitchen area with a stove, refrigerator, table and chairs, a living room, and dining room

Iceman House

Floors: 3 + basement

Total Occupancy: 11

Room Types: Singles and doubles

Program: Classical Studies

Special Features: Laundry facilities; a kitchen area with a stove, refrigerator, table and chairs, a living room

Johnson House

Floors: 2 + basement

Total Occupancy: 9

Room Types: Singles and doubles

Program: French

Special Features: Laundry facilities; a kitchen area with a stove, refrigerator, table and chairs, a living room

Kate House

Floors: 3 + basement

Total Occupancy: 15

Room Types: Singles

Program: Science and Hummanities

Special Features: Laundry facilities; a kitchen area with a stove, refrigerator, table and chairs, a living room

Kennedy Apartments

Floors: 1 + basement, 4 sections

Total Occupancy: 16

Room Types: Singles and doubles

Program: French

Special Features: Laundry facilities; a kitchen area with a stove, refrigerator, table and chairs in each section, a living room, and dining room in each section

Kieffer House

Floors: 2 + basement

Total Occupancy: 9

Room Types: Singles and doubles

Program: French

Special Features: Laundry facilities; a kitchen area with a stove, refrigerator, table and chairs, a living room, and dining room

Lewis House

Floors: 3 + basement

Total Occupancy: 9

Room Types: Singles and doubles

Program: French

Special Features: Laundry facilities; a kitchen area with a stove, refrigerator, table and chairs, a living room, and dining room

McDavitt House

Floors: 2 + basement

Total Occupancy: 5

Room Types: Singles and doubles

Program: French

Special Features: Laundry facilities; a kitchen area with a stove, refrigerator, table and chairs, a living room

Miller Manor

Floors: 2 + basement

Total Occupancy: 30

Room Types: Singles, doubles, and triples

Program: French

Special Features: Laundry facilities; a kitchen area with a stove, refrigerator, table and chairs, a living room

Monyer House

Floors: 3 + basement

Total Occupancy: 12

Room Types: Singles, doubles, and triples

Program: French

Special Features: Laundry facilities; a kitchen area with a stove, refrigerator, table and chairs, a living room, and dining room

Morris House

Floors: 1 + basement

Total Occupancy: 4

Room Types: Doubles

(Morris House, continued)

Program: French

Special Features: Laundry facilities; a kitchen area with a stove, refrigerator, table and chairs, a living room

Reed House

Floors: 2 + basement

Total Occupancy: 11

Room Types: Singles and doubles

Program: French

Special Features: Laundry facilities; a kitchen area with a stove, refrigerator, table and chairs, a living room

Richardson House

Floors: 2 + basement

Total Occupancy: 8

Room Types: Doubles

Program: French

Special Features: Laundry facilities; a kitchen area with a stove, refrigerator, table and chairs, a living room, and dining room

Rickett House

Floors: 2 + basement

Total Occupancy: 5

Room Types: Singles and doubles

Program: French

Special Features: Laundry facilities; a kitchen area with a stove, refrigerator, table and chairs, a living room

Schlabach House

Floors: 2 + basement

Total Occupancy: 5

Room Types: Singles and doubles

Program: French

Special Features: Laundry facilities; a kitchen area with a stove, refrigerator, table and chairs, a living room, dining room, informal parlor

Scot Cottage

Floors: 2 + basement

Total Occupancy: 15

Room Types: Singles and doubles

Program: French

Special Features: Laundry facilities; a kitchen area with a stove, refrigerator, table and chairs, a large living room

Shearer House

Floors: 2 + basement

Total Occupancy: 9

Room Types: Singles and doubles

Program: French

Special Features: Laundry facilities, a kitchen area with a stove, refrigerator, table and chairs, a living room and dining room

Stadium House

Floors: 2 + basement

Total Occupancy: 9

Room Types: Singles

Program: French

(Stadium House, continued)

Special Features: Laundry facilities; a kitchen area with a stove, refrigerator, table and chairs, a living room, and dining room

Troyer House

Floors: 2 + basement

Total Occupancy: 13

Room Types: Singles, doubles, and triples

Program: French

Special Features: Laundry facilities, a kitchen area with a stove and refrigerator

Weber House

Floors: 2 + basement

Total Occupancy: 11

Room Types: Singles and doubles

Program: French

Special Features: Laundry facilities; a kitchen area with a stove, refrigerator, table and chairs, a living room

Westminster House

Floors: 3 + basement

Total Occupancy: 31

Room Types: Singles, doubles, and triples

Program: French

Special Features: Laundry facilities; a kitchen area with a stove, a living room, dining room, and study room

→

Yost House

Floors: 2 + basement

Total Occupancy: 6

Room Types: Singles and doubles

Program: French

Special Features: Laundry facilities; a kitchen area with a stove, refrigerator, table and chairs, a living room, and dining room

Did You Know?

A few years ago, an alumnus donated money to create **grill and patio areas** outside of every dormitory on campus! Students use these areas often, having weekend picnics with friends, or just sitting outside in the wooden chairs under a tree and reading.

Bed Type

Twin extra-long (39"x 80"); some lofts, some bunk-beds

Cleaning Service?

Yes. The College's custodial staff cleans the restrooms and public areas in both the dormitories and houses five days a week. On weekends, they come in briefly for basic maintenance, such as taking out the restroom trash.

You Get

Each room is furnished with beds, desks, closets or wardrobes, dressers, desk chairs, bookcases or bookshelves, cable TV jack, Ethernet connections, and free campus and local phone calls.

Available for Rent

Summer storage space

Also Available

Chemical-free living, smoke-free living, quiet option, special-interest groups

Students Speak Out On...
Campus Housing

"K-town is the best dorm. Well, if you can manage a language suite in Luce, that's even better. Otherwise, Kenarden is great. I've also lived in Holden for three years, and I love the centrality; five minutes to food, work, and class."

Q "I think Armington, Bissman, and Stevenson are prison cells. I really like Compton and Wagner; the rooms are nice, and you have a lot of storage space. Holden also has a very good location."

Q "You know, everyone always complains about Holden Annex, and it gets a bad rap. But that dorm is in a great location and has really decent-sized rooms that are fine inside, except for the missing closet doors. I mean, sure, we may joke that it could burn down in four minutes if someone set one end of it alight, but truthfully, no one knows if that's true. I liked the Annex. It was kind of fun."

Q "Most of the dorms are very nice. The rooms are big, the bathrooms are clean, and there are very nice large public lounges. Armington Hall has very small rooms, but is fairly new and redone. Holden Hall is popular as it is close to everything on campus. Douglass Hall is the oldest on campus and has very nice big rooms, as well as Kenarden Lodge, which houses upperclass students and was redone in the past 10 years or so."

Q "I've lived in small houses for three years now, and I love them. **Volunteering for the community has been great**, and I love that I'm able to have a kitchen and living room—basically an apartment—with all of my best friends! Weber, Westminster, Scot Cottage, Miller Manor, Corner, Colonial, and Troyer are all great houses, just to name a few."

Q "The dorms are generally nice, although some rooms seem like closets compared to others. **Holden Hall has the best location**, although it tends to be noisy."

Q "I live in Compton (the all-female dorm), and I love it. **Douglass and Andrews are cool**, though, both inside and out."

Q "Babcock is a great dorm to live in with an awesome community sense. The bathrooms are clean, and even though the furniture is kind of old, **the hardwood floors are beautiful**. Babcock and Kenarden all the way!"

Q "Don't stay in Bissman, Stevenson, or Wagner. The rest all have their advantages and disadvantages. And **don't be afraid of program dorms** or the small house programs; they're really neat."

Q "We have pretty large rooms at Wooster. Kenarden Lodge and Luce Hall are the best dorms by far. Douglass and Babcock are really great, too. **Avoid Stevenson and Armington like the plague**."

Q **"The dorms aren't too bad**. The only one I'd truly try to avoid is Holden Annex—it's been 'temporary housing' since 1921!"

Q "**Most of the dorms are really nice**, and they're pretty spacious in comparison with other colleges. Compton, Douglass, and Kenarden are the nicest."

Q "I like the dorms in general, but the small houses are awesome, too. Get your friends together and **get a cool program house**; you'll definitely appreciate it in the end."

Q "The dorms are fine, but in my last two years, I really enjoyed living in a house that the campus owned. It allowed more space and was homier. The nice dorms are Kenarden and Luce primarily, and Holden Hotel. **I think the worst has to be Bissman**."

The College Prowler Take On...
Campus Housing

Residential Life and Housing have outdone themselves in terms of providing a wide variety of on-campus living options. Most students are satisfied with the rooms they get every year, and the program dorms are thriving parts of the community. In terms of the physical structures of the dormitories and houses themselves, three-fourths of the students live in a residence hall that they love. The dorms are well maintained, and exude an architectural grace that students say makes them feel like they are living in mansions.

Two of the four dorms on campus that students like the least have been renovated in the past three years. The displeasure about the buildings comes not from the quality of living, but the quantity. Some of the older dorms on campus, Holden especially, are also badly in need of renovation, which has been put on hold again and again. Overall, students seem satisfied with their housing situations.

B+

The College Prowler® Grade on

Campus Housing: B+

A high Campus Housing grade indicates that dorms are clean, well-maintained, and spacious. Other determining factors include variety of dorms, proximity to classes, and social atmosphere.

Off-Campus Housing

The Lowdown On...
Off-Campus Housing

Undergrads in Off-Campus Housing:

1%

Rules Regulating Off-Campus Housing:

Off-campus living is considered a special housing option. Only seniors and juniors are eligible to apply for this privilege, and only a very small percentage of students are afforded it.

Best Time to Look for a Place:

The semester before you want to live off campus

Average Rent For:

1BR Apt.: $400/month
2BR Apt.: $500/month
3BR Apt.: $600/month

Popular Areas:

Anywhere around the edges of campus

➜

→

**For Assistance
Contact:**
Residential Life & Housing
(330) 263-2498

Students Speak Out On...
Off-Campus Housing

"I've never looked into it, but I doubt it's worth it, because living on campus is a learning experience in itself. You have to take baby steps before you jump right into paying your own rent and gas bills."

Q "It's not worth it; get the meals! You feel disconnected from the college, and **it's a pain in the butt to get to classes**."

Q "**It is nearly impossible to move off campus** because of the comprehensive fee, but those who do say that it is a great deal cheaper."

Q "Everyone pretty much lives on campus **all four years**."

Q "I lived off campus last year, and while I loved having the freedom to do what I wanted without worrying about the College, security, or any crap like that, but **I did miss the community of the dorms**. It's worth it if you're making the plunge into the real world the next year, but it depends on what you want to take out of your college experience."

Q "You have to apply, and **underclassmen cannot live off campus**. I lived off campus my senior year, and it was one of the best decisions I made."

Q "Housing on campus can be a headache, so if you can find a nice, cheap place off campus, **it might be worth your time trying**."

Q "Only juniors and seniors can live off campus, and I don't think it is that worth it. If you want a house, get a volunteer house together. You get the same amenities, but someone comes to clean the place. Also, it's difficult to get the go ahead to live off campus. When all of your friends are on campus, **it hurts your social life**."

Q "I don't know. **Some people say it's a good idea**, but those people are very few and far between."

Q "Off-campus living is very inconvenient. I've heard that not only is it expensive, but it's hard, because **you have to petition the dean** or something and not many people are granted the request. Most likely it's not worth it."

The College Prowler Take On...
Off-Campus Housing

Off-campus housing at Wooster is basically nonexistent. Residential Life and Housing programs have covered all the bases, from large hall dormitories to suite-like dorms to small volunteer program houses and everything in between. Very few students have ever lived off campus, and those who do say that they are on their own when searching for apartments. It was difficult to find anyone willing to speak on the subject, merely because no one has ever experienced off-campus living at Wooster.

For those few students who have lived off campus, some say that it was the best experience of their lives, while others say they miss the feel of the campus community. Simply put, while off-campus living is not necessary, if you really want to do it choose wisely.

The College Prowler® Grade on
Off-Campus Housing: D

A high grade in Off-Campus Housing indicates that apartments are of high quality, close to campus, affordable, and easy to secure.

Diversity

The Lowdown On...
Diversity

Native American:	**White:**
0%	86%
Asian American:	**International:**
1%	7%
African American:	**Out-of-State:**
5%	45%
Hispanic:	
1%	

Political Activity

Many students are politically and socially liberal. Wooster has had several peaceful protests recently which provokes the largely conservative town. There is definitely a percentage of people on campus working hard for social activism. Other than that, students can be pretty apathetic or just loose interest quickly.

Gay Pride

Students who are members of Allies & Queers, the dominant group for gays on campus, dedicated to promoting awareness on campus. For the most part, gays are accepted, although not entirely considering that Wooster is a conservative area.

Most Popular Religions

Wooster was originally a Presbyterian college, although it is now nondenominational. There are many Christian groups on campus, as well as a Jewish group called Hillel. Also present are several Muslim, Hindi, and other religious groups.

Economic Status

The major economic group at the College seems to be middle class. Within that sphere, there are many differences, and a large gap sometimes appears between the lower, middle, and upper. Nothing so bad that it ever stands out, except when students discuss family life at home.

Minority Clubs

There are many active minority groups on campus, from the International Student Association, which hosts Indian dinners and movies, as well as many events from other cultures, to the Men of Harambee and the Women of Images, two examples of cultural/social groups on campus that provide many events to educate the campus community.

Students Speak Out On...
Diversity

> "I'd like to think of Wooster as a school that is pretty big on diversity; it's actually one of the reasons I'm here. I wanted to attend a school with a large percentage of students from other countries."

Q "Wooster is not diverse enough. **There isn't even remotely equal representation**. That is definitely a weak point of the College."

Q "I would say Wooster is pretty diverse. I am friends with several people from other countries. **You can find diversity** if you want to find it."

Q "**We have a wide range of international students** and a diverse student body both racially and culturally."

Q "**Wooster is fairly diverse** for a small liberal arts college in Ohio. The College puts in a lot of effort to draw from all sorts of people around the country and world."

Q "I don't think Wooster is very diverse at all; I have found that **some international students are reluctant to assimilate**. This could be a result of the fact that there are large clusters of students from a small number of countries."

Q "**There are a lot of international students** and a decent black student population for an area so small."

Q "The campus is diverse in comparison to other schools in the conference, with quite a few people from the Asian region, but **it's primarily white upper-middle class.**"

Q "Being a minority, I'd say that **this campus could stand to see more diversity**. If you are a minority reading this, we need you!"

Q "Considering that I am from India, I would say that Wooster's diversity is not bad. **I have found many friends here**, both American and international."

Q "**The diversity is as diverse as the larger country**. You can be easily isolated, or very involved and included."

Q "The campus is not very diverse across race, but we do have a lot of international students. **The College is trying to increase diversity**."

The College Prowler Take On...
Diversity

While students feel that there's diversity at Wooster, they tend to gauge that factor by quality, not quantity. If you look at the numbers, Wooster can be seen as predominantly white and isolated. However, when you see the impact that the diversity has made on the College's campus, you understand that while diversity is small, the minority students are strong. They tend to stand out because they involve the entire campus in events. For example, last spring, one of the well-attended and school-sponsored events was an African step-dance troupe, which attracted roughly 400 people. Also, the percentage of international students that attend Wooster is extremely high for a small liberal arts college in Ohio, and they play prominent roles in the campus community.

Overall, students say what really makes the difference is how much you want diversity to be a part of your life at Wooster. If you are looking to learn about other cultures, you can find your niche very easily. If you want to stay with what makes you comfortable, that is freely available as well. However, achieving diversity is something that is not entirely subjective; you can't immerse yourself in diverse cultures if they are not there.

The College Prowler® Grade on

Diversity: D+

A high grade in Diversity indicates that ethnic minorities and international students have a notable presence on campus and that students of different economic backgrounds, religious beliefs, and sexual preferences are well-represented.

Guys & Girls

The Lowdown On...
Guys & Girls

Men Undergrads:
47%

Women Undergrads:
53%

Birth Control Available?

Yes. The Longbrake Wellness Center must provide women with a free gynecologist exam before the pill can be administered, but most prices for it are around $15. Condoms are given out by Residential Assistants and the Wellness Center.

Social Scene

Students are very interactive at Wooster. Because it is a small college, everyone is involved in everything, and people know one another through the different activities they do. Another important thing about students at Wooster is that they can't be categorized. They range from rich to poor, liberal to conservative, athletes to hippies, and everything in between.

Hookups or Relationships?

Relationships are more popular than random hookups at Wooster. While hookups do happen, they don't happen regularly because it is such a small campus. As one student said, "You can't make out at a party or have one night stands without half of the campus knowing about it the next day." One thing you will find at Wooster is a lot of casual dating, which is a nice balance between the two extremes.

Best Place to Meet Guys/Girls

Most students at Wooster meet through their classes, jobs, or the extracurriculars they do on campus. However, probably one of the best places to meet people tends to be at parties or through friends, not unlike the way the real world works. Just never try to date people in the same dorm as you because it can lead to very awkward living situations.

Did You Know?

Top Three Places to Find Hotties:
1. Any house party on campus
2. The College Underground
3. In class!

Top Five Places to Hook Up:
1. Roof of McGaw Chapel
2. The 9-hole golf course
3. Your room
4. Dorm lounges
5. The libraries

Dress Code

Casual—that is the number one word for how students dress at Wooster. While you won't find an obscene number of kids going to class in their pajamas (unless it's at 8 a.m., and then that's condoned), you also won't find that many kids going all out in style. Sometimes, you'll catch sight of a girl wobbling along on Kenneth Cole stilettos and tripping over the bricks, but mainly, jeans and casual shirts are the norm. Wooster girls and guys don't really care about the latest fashion trends, but somehow usually end up wearing them, from great scarves to pull your hair back with to fun Goodwill T-shirts with funny, local names on them. Make a trip to Goodwill. It's a must.

Students Speak Out On...
Guys & Girls

"There are hot guys and ugly guys. There's very little in between. There are some genuinely nice ones, though. They are a little hard to find sometimes."

Q "Well, I cannot speak to the attractiveness of Wooster's girls, but the guys are pretty good looking. **There aren't many head-turners**, but most guys get more attractive as you get to know them."

Q "There are some really smart girls here and some really ditzy girls. And **I never knew guys could be ditzy**."

Q "**There's a good mix of people on campus,** a little of everything. For the most part, people can all socialize together."

Q "I heard we were named in *Playboy* as one of the 10th ugliest colleges for girls or something like that, but I bet every college says that, because my cousin goes to Kent State, and they have the same rumor there. I think that it depends. **I see plenty of cute girls and guys**, and some ugly ones, too!"

Q "Surprisingly, **there are some hot guys** on this campus."

Q "**The boys and girls are cute but preppy**, so if you like that look, then yes, good-looking people are here."

Q "Students here tend to be pretty diverse in their personal styles, so **it depends on what you're looking for**. I'd say yes, depending on personal preference, there are hot girls and guys at Woo."

Q "The student body is very diverse, ranging from the frat boy/sorority girl look to the hippies. Are they hot? **You're here to get an education—not a mate**."

Q "We have so many people at Wooster that you can't really generalize. Sure, **I think we're a good-looking bunch**, but I wouldn't say that there are many that stand out in the crowd, either way—both ugly and pretty."

Q "**There are more girls on campus then guys**, but like anywhere, you have hotties and not-so-hotties."

Q "I always thought the guys at Wooster were nice looking overall, and I believe that generally everyone is rather friendly. Of course, there are people that might be hard to approach and are not the most gorgeous. **They say beauty is inner**, and if you like a close-knit community, you'll find someone who values that also."

The College Prowler Take On...
Guys & Girls

Students at Wooster tend to be interested in many different activities and people. At Woo, you wouldn't be surprised to hear that a guy who plays ultimate Frisbee and is a biology major can also be the editor-in-chief of the student newspaper and be involved in the dance concerts. That's just how eclectic they are.

Wooster students are also not very concerned with looks. While they'll admit that some people are nicer looking than others, this is not a campus that you step onto and immediately think everyone else has stepped off of the cover of *Vogue*. The general consensus is that most people on campus are nice-looking girl/guy next door types, with an average amount of pretty people and not-so-pretty people. Basically, there are a fair amount of beautiful people and not-so-beautiful people, just like any other campus. Also, like other average college campuses, Woo has its fair number of promiscuous and not-so-promiscuous people.

The College Prowler® Grade on
Guys: B-

A high grade for Guys indicates that the male population on campus is attractive, smart, friendly, and engaging, and that the school has a decent ratio of guys to girls.

The College Prowler® Grade on
Girls: B

A high grade for Girls not only implies that the women on campus are attractive, smart, friendly, and engaging, but also that there is a fair ratio of girls to guys.

Athletics

The Lowdown On...
Athletics

Athletic Division:
NCAA Division III

Conference:
North Coast Athletic

School Mascot:
The Fighting Scots

**Males Playing
Varsity Sports:**
309 (36%)

**Females Playing
Varsity Sports:**
207 (21%)

➡

Men's Varsity Teams:

Baseball
Basketball
Cross-Country
Football
Golf
Indoor Track
Lacrosse
Soccer
Swimming & Diving
Tennis
Track & Field

Women's Varsity Teams:

Basketball
Cross-Country
Field Hockey
Indoor Track
Lacrosse
Soccer
Softball
Swimming & Diving
Tennis
Track & Field
Volleyball

Club Sports:

Badminton
Cheerleading
Cricket
Fencing
Personal Foul (dance team)
Table Tennis
Ultimate Frisbee
Volleyball

Intramurals:

Basketball
Billiards
Bowling
Flag Football
Floor Hockey
Golf
Kickboxing
Soccer
Softball
Swimming
Table Tennis
Tennis
Ultimate Frisbee
Volleyball

Getting Tickets

General ticket sales allow for one free ticket per student, with discounts for alumni. Most events are free to everyone.

Best Place to Take a Walk

Friendship Park, on the west side of campus, Around the campus (it takes maybe twenty minutes to circle the grounds), Downtown Wooster, or to Hop Hing or Blockbuster and back

Most Popular Sports

In varsity sports, the football and basketball teams have very large followings, and they do very well every year. Many of the IM sports are popular, such as soccer, volleyball, lacrosse, and floor hockey.

Overlooked Teams

The cricket club is a band of very enthusiastic players, who have been trying for several years to get recognition from the school for consistently beating Haverford's varsity cricket team.

Armington Physical Education Center

This building houses the Timken Gymnasium, which provides intercollegiate basketball seating for 3,420 and serves as a multi-station area for classes, intramural sports, and recreational activities. A wrestling room and a conditioning room were completely renovated and converted into the Swigart Fitness Center. The building contains a six-lane swimming pool, a multi-purpose gymnasium, an exercise physiology laboratory, a coeducational training room, locker rooms, equipment and laundry rooms, a classroom, the Women's Recreation Association office, and an administrative wing.

Did You Know?

Wooster has won the North Coast Athletic Conference's **All-Sports Trophy** five times in the conference's 18-year history. Wooster teams and individuals also competed in NCAA postseason competition in three different sports in 2005.

Students Speak Out On...
Athletics

{ **"Varsity sports take over some of my friends lives. They get a lot of support from peers, alumni, and faculty, but sports aren't as big a priority as they would be at a D-I school. IM sports get a lot or participants, though."**

Q "**Varsity sports aren't too big**; they are played for fun and not to make money. There are a few IM sports teams I know of, such as soccer, which are fairly popular."

Q "**IM and varsity sports are both big** on this campus and just as competitive. Many people of very many different levels of ability like to play."

Q "**Sports range medium at Wooster**. Varsity sports depend on how well the sport is doing in the season. Wooster's men's basketball is by far the most popular. IM is pretty popular, too, and can be great fun without the practice, with such sports as softball, floor hockey, and Frisbee."

Q "Football is a really well-attended sport, but we are a Division III school, so some people have never been to a game. **Many people do IM sports here**. Those are really fun."

Q "Varsity and IMs are a big part of many students' lives here at Wooster. **Major events are football, field hockey, and soccer**. They also draw the attention of many people in the community."

Q "Varsity sports and **sports in general don't seem to be too big** on this campus, though IM sports cause lots of excitement with the non-athletes."

Q "Academics come before sports, and I've never really felt that they have been oppressively important. IM sports are huge, however, and **the participants can get disgruntled**."

Q "IM sports are great—do as many as you can, especially floor hockey. **Varsity sports are a little incestuous**—if that's what you want and what you're dedicated to, however, you can be as focused and single-minded as you so desire."

Q "**Sports are big on campus**, but you don't have to participate. Even though a lot of people are involved, it is not a 'sports' school; people are here for academics primarily."

Q "If you're into sports, **there's plenty to get involved** with somehow, either varsity or IM. If you're not, there are plenty of other things to do."

Q "It seems that **a lot of people participate in sports**. IMs are pretty involved, and there's no real commitment or competition, so it's fun to get out and play."

Q "I love sports, so **I like to go to the games**. Most are well attended, and IM is always fun!"

Q "**I love IM sports**. I had a lot of fun playing softball and basketball, and it's a great way to meet new people."

Q "Personally, I follow IM sports closer than varsity sports simply because **all my friends play IM**. There seems to be a wonderful turnout for varsity games, though, and the town really gets involved, as well."

The College Prowler Take On...
Athletics

Wooster's athletics are well respected by other colleges in the conference. Most sports teams are very competitive in the conference, if not nationally, and most teams get fairly decent support from the student body and the school in general. Needless to say, sports teams at Woo are not only well represented, but most students say that they feel sports and academics at Wooster are treated equally. This is not a jock school, but a school where students come to learn and still pursue their favorite activities. Even while academics are number one, sports don't lag here.

For example, in the past two years, the women's swim team has been 7th and then 5th in the nation in the division, and the football team and men's soccer finished in 3rd place in the conference in 2002. The men's basketball team went to the Division III Final Four game for the first time ever in 2003, taking 3rd place overall. Although IMs are popular here, this is still a D-III school, which means that varsity sports aren't top-notch. However, some events still draw in the large crowds.

The College Prowler® Grade on

Athletics: B

A high grade in Athletics indicates that students have school spirit, that sports programs are respected, that games are well-attended, and that intramurals are a prominent part of student life.

The Lowdown On...
Nightlife

Club and Bar Prowler:
Popular Nightlife Spots:

Club Crawler:

Nightclubs in Wooster are virtually nonexistent.

On Campus:

The fact that Wooster has an on-campus bar is rare among campuses its size. They are very fortunate, or unfortunate depending on how you look at it, to have the Underground. This campus also has a full liquor license, even though they don't completely utilize it.

The College Underground
(Below Kittredge Dining Hall)

Both a club and a bar, the Underground is where you will find many of your friends on the weekends. It is open Fridays and Saturdays for happy hour, and then

➡

(The College Underground, continued)

everyone will start to arrive to dance. Usually, if you are 21 or not, the UG is a place to start out your night before moving off to other parties. On nights when there are no parties to be found on campus, everyone flocks to the UG, and then it feels like a huge, sweaty dance club; almost like a real place you would go to in the city.

Off-Campus:
The Decades

1865 Beall Ave.

(330) 262-5111

A bar and dance room all rolled into one, the Decades is about the only place around Wooster that can even be vaguely called a dance club. They feature a large dance area, a game room with lots of pool tables, darts, air hockey and foosball, and a sports lounge. You must be 21 to get into the Decades, be dressed properly (no backwards hats, boys), and they have a small cover charge. Wednesday is College Night (18 and over), where you'll find pitchers for $3.50 and $1 drafts.

Bar Prowler:

On Campus:
The College Underground
(Below Kittredge Dining Hall)

On the bar end of the UG, you'll find many great beers on tap for great prices. The beers on tap range from $.75 to $1.50 or $2, and the bottles are anywhere from $1 to $3. The Underground's special is $2.50 plastic cups with $1.00 refills for the rest of the year. The cups have various sports teams on them, allowing students to choose their favorites.

Off-Campus:
Applebee's Grill & Bar

3989 Burbank Rd.

(330) 345-8900

Applebee's is your basic family restaurant with a bar in the center of the place, featuring great food and expensive drinks. With many different selections on tap, Applebee's is also known for its specialty drinks, such as margaritas, mud slides, and pina coladas.

Buffalo Wild Wings

4122 Burbank Rd.

(330) 264-2299

BW's is a very famous New York chain. New to the area, it is a sports bar that features barbecued buffalo wild wings, hence the name. They also feature televisions lining the walls. Students say the atmosphere is great, very laid-back and casual.

CW Burgerstein's Great Sandwich Works

359 W Liberty St.

(330) 264-6263

Another grill in Wooster, CW's is in the basement of TJ's restaurant. It's a sandwich shop with all-American food and a laid-back atmosphere where you can watch television, eat some food, and order a few drinks from the full bar.

El Campesino

177 W Milltown Rd.

(330) 345-6263

Yet another restaurant with a bar, El Campesino's claim to fame is that the waiters can barely speak English, and the margarita glasses are large enough to swim in.

(El Campesino, continued)

Buy a $9 margarita, and you are set for the night. Not only is the food great, but the alcohol is cheap.

Gemini Lounge

981 Grosjean Rd.

(330) 263-4411

Although it might be a bit sketchy, the Gemini/Becky's has some endearing qualities, such as the Native American busts mounted behind the fake marble bar. The bar features a dance floor, pool tables, a foosball table, a pinball machine, and an extensive jukebox. A small menu of snacks includes jalapeno poppers which the regulars say are top-quality. The selection is mainly domestic beers, such as PBR, Busch, Miller, and Rolling Rock. The cherry bombs (maraschino cherries soaked in Bacardi151) are three for a dollar. Every Friday, a band performs after 10 p.m.

Murphy's Market Grill

234 S Market St.

(330) 262-0741

The Market Grill is a long, narrow bar with a four-sided main counter in the center. Two pool tables are in the back corners, and the bartenders wear leather vests. The bar has a very blue-collar look; you might even hobnob with the locals. However, students say the prices are great, with beer served in 16 ounce mason jars for $1.50, bottles for $2.50, and cans for $.75.

The Olde Jaol Tavern

215 N Walnut St.

(330) 262-3333

The Olde Jaol is probably Wooster's classiest bar. They offer quality food and a large selection of both domestic and import beers on tap. They also have a moderate selection of wines and a full bar with what some students refer to as excellent shots. There are indoor and outdoor seating options, with industrial strength heaters outside to keep you warm even in the coldest months.

Seattle's Coffee House

131 N Market St.

(330) 262-2998

Seattle's is a coffee house prone to serving upscale beers on tap, such as Guinness, Harp, Bass, Sam Adams, Heineken, Great Lakes, and Sierra Nevada. If you want to test a beer before committing, Seattle's will happily whip out a complimentary four-ounce sampler glass. There are tables where some students play checkers, as well as a small area to relax in cushy sofa chairs. The atmosphere is very mellow, with bands performing on the weekends for a $3 cover charge.

Tumbleweed Southwest Mesquite Grill & Bar

4147 Burbank Rd.

(330) 345-1550

Another restaurant and bar in Wooster, the Tumbleweed features Margarita Mondays, which is a big deal for college students here. Margaritas for $1 on Monday.

Student Favorites:

The College Underground

The Decades

Murphy's Market Grill

The Old Joal Tavern

**Cheapest Place
to Get a Drink:**

Club Veemara-Knights

The College Underground

**Favorite Drinking
Games:**

Beer Pong

Card Games

Century Club

Quarters

Bars Close At:

1 or 2 a.m.

What to Do if You're Not 21

Party on campus, in any dorm room or small house. Get upperclassmen to buy you alcohol and teach yourself how to bartend for your friends.

House Parties

House parties are a big part of Wooster. If you aren't hanging out at the Underground or a dorm room, chances are you're at a party at a small house. Every year, the groups on campus switch houses, so your best bet is to keep one ear to the ground, and soon enough, you'll find out which places are the best ones to party at.

Organization Parties

There are a few groups on campus that traditionally have great parties. One of these is Greenhouse, the student environmental house on campus. Not only are they friendly people, but they recycle their beer cans. Also, the Crandalls, the truest hippie fraternity you'll ever see, host Baachannalia every year at an off-campus site called Beck's Family Campground. It's a huge party with 80-plus kegs and jam bands from all over the nation, estimating roughly 1,000 to 2,000 people every year. People under 21 are allowed in, but not to drink.

Frat Parties

See the Greek section!

Did You Know?

Every year, **the Betas have a Beta Run** from one end of the campus to the other in the frigid cold, slushy snow. Unsuspecting first-years are dragged out of their dorms to be cheering squads.

Students Speak Out On...
Nightlife

"A lot of the parties on campus are sponsored by the Greek groups. There are some small house parties, but no parties seem to get very large, except for the ones at the Zetas' off-campus house."

Q "Parties are fun. They are generally all-inclusive, and everyone is usually pretty welcoming. **The UG is fun, but not as a final destination**. I don't usually head off campus to party, so I don't know about the stuff that's out there."

Q "Haha. Bars off campus? Right. Most of that stuff is on campus. The college has a bar for students, **there's usually a keg at the frats**, and the small house parties will either be cans of Beast, or cheap hard liquor if the party's semi-private."

Q "**The parties on campus are great**, but are often broken down by security (because they have nothing else to do)."

Q "There are some really good parties on campus—**lots of drinks and nice people**. The only parties I have found to be incredibly boring are the Greek parties."

Q "Bars and clubs off campus? **We have those**? We have the campus Underground, which is our only on-campus club, and there are house parties on the weekends."

Q "Parties on campus are great. **Weber House and Greenhouse have awesome parties**, and many do theme parties, like 'Come and Get Lai-ed' or the 'Ironic Hipster' themes."

Q "The campus club/bar is the Underground, which is okay, but not great. I really don't go to parties, clubs, or bars. If I go out, it's to a friend's room. **If I drink, it's in a friend's room**."

Q "**The parties on campus are really good** and a lot of people come out. I am not familiar with any of the off-campus nightlife."

Q "The parties on campus are usually not that huge or formal. They are basically a lot of people getting drunk. The bars/clubs off campus aren't that intriguing. There is Club Veemara-Knight's, which is neat on Halloween, but if you're a partier, **I'd recommend driving to the bars in Akron**."

Q "Parties suck on campus, unless you like frat/sorority parties. **If you want to do some real clubbing, go to Cleveland**."

Q "**The huge parties are few and far between**, but very fun. Going off campus is scary."

Q "**Bars and clubs are shared with the townspeople** of Wooster. It keeps things interesting. As for parties on campus, the best ones are when five or ten people would just sit around and hang out."

Q "Wooster parties take some time getting used to. Since it's a small campus, you always run into people you know, and word travels fast about where parties are. **Arriving anywhere before 10:30 is a big risk**, since you might be the first there."

Q "**The parties are small** and more laid-back. People can get crazy sometimes, but it usually doesn't get out of hand. Most people stay on campus on the weekends."

The College Prowler Take On...
Nightlife

While there aren't many prime choices for partying off campus, students don't seem to notice. They find plenty of activities to keep themselves entertained on campus. Parties on campus may be hosted by a specific group, such as the theater people, the Greenhouse, or a fraternity or sorority. As freshmen, students normally go to the larger parties on campus, including the fraternities and sororities. They also frequent the Underground much more than upperclassmen. However, as you meet more upperclassmen on campus, your knowledge will expand, and you'll soon be checking out the larger house parties both on and off campus. By junior year, weekends consist of house parties, theme parties, pre-parties, and every once in a while, you'll hit up the Underground out of boredom. Once you and all of your friends turn 21, you'll discover that you need to eat dinner at 5 p.m. so that you can get the full effect of happy hour at the UG before heading out to other events.

If you aren't into the alcohol scene, don't think you can't party. College is not a place where strangers pressure you, and many people find they have just as much fun sober as they do while drinking. The key is to like the atmosphere and the people at a party, and you'll have fun no matter what your state of mind is. Also, there are great activities like going to Scot Lanes and Common Grounds.

B

The College Prowler® Grade on
Nightlife: B

A high grade in Nightlife indicates that there are many bars and clubs in the area that are easily accessible and affordable. Other determining factors include the number of options for the under-21 crowd and the prevalence of house parties.

Greek Life

The Lowdown On...
Greek Life

Number of Fraternities:
5

Number of Sororities:
6

Undergrad Men in Fraternities:
8%

Undergrad Women in Sororities:
12%

→

Fraternities on Campus:

Beta Kappa Phi
Phi Delta Sigma
Phi Omega Sigma
Phi Sigma Alpha
Xi Chi Psi

Sororities on Campus:

Alpha Gamma Phi
Delta Phi Alpha
Delta Theta Psi
Epsilon Kappa Omicron
Pi Kappa
Zeta Phi Gamma

Multicultural Colonies:

Dene House
Women of IMAGES
Men of Harambee

Honorary Colonies:

Eta Sigma Phi
Lambda Pi Eta
Phi Alpha Theta
Phi Beta Kappa
Psi Chi

Other Greek Organizations:

Council of Social Organizations
Inter-Greek Council

> **"It doesn't dominate the social scene. People within the Greek system are still good friends with people who are independents, and everyone stays happy."**

Q "There are no national sororities or fraternities at Wooster. **The campus organizations are there if you want them**, but they don't dominate the scene."

Q "Some of my best friends are Greeks, and some of my worst enemies are, too. It just depends. I think that **the Alpha Gamms are really nice girls**, the EKOs are, too. The Thetas can be snotty, but overall, they are decent. The Zetas are just big partiers."

Q "**Greek life doesn't dominate the social scene**. It doesn't get the most attention on campus."

Q "**The Greeks are small but active in Wooster**. As a member of a sorority that I love, I would have to say that it really depends on the group. I enjoy that we are local, because I feel that I really get to know my girls better than I would if it were a huge university sorority. The Thetas volunteer regularly in the community, and we are a very close-knit group."

Q "Yeah, we have Greeks. **Usually they do dumb things**, though, like set their dorms on fire and paddle each other senseless—and get caught, eventually."

Q "Honestly, I have no interest whatsoever in the Greek scene. I have gone to the Omega house twice, and both times I left after 10 minutes—**it was so boring**."

Q "Greek life doesn't dominate, but **it's a huge part of the social scene**, as the different Greek organizations are really the only ones hosting social gatherings and parties."

Q "**I'm more or less anti-Greek.** There seems to be a small representation, but the people who are a part of Greek life seem to enjoy it."

Q "The Xi Chi's are the band geeks, the Betas are your traditional big partiers, and the **Delts are the funny, kind of weird kids**. You have everything in the frats, so there's always someone you'd get to know well and like."

Q "I don't even know who is or isn't in what club or section. **They aren't even national chapters**! Maybe it's just not my scene, but our Greek life doesn't dominate Wooster's social life."

Q "Greek life doesn't dominate the scene at all. Yes, they are the primary ones that have parties and are obvious during pledging season, but other than that, you have your own option to be or not be Greek. With only about one in five people in the Greek system, **you can fit in anywhere**."

Q "**I wouldn't say the Greeks dominate**. Like any organization there is stereotyping, but I know many people in frats/sororities, such as the Xi Chis and the Alpha Gammas, and they are cool."

Q "Greek life is there and only dominates in the sense that they have off-campus parties. **All parties are open**, and you can go for four years never attending a Greek party and still have fun."

The College Prowler Take On...
Greek Life

Greek life does not dominate the social scene. While there are fraternities and sororities on campus, they do not seem to make a big impression on the social situation. There are Greek parties, and they are usually open to everyone on campus. In recent years, the Greek system has gotten a bad rap for several hazing incidents in different groups, which occurred throughout the '90s up to the present, and got them kicked off campus. Also, the College has been reasonably harsh to the groups, setting up difficult rules, such as setting a maximum of all campus parties they must host a year, requiring them to pay the Underground staff to work their party, and stamping every student at the door.

Students feel that being in a Greek group isn't important at all. Those who do participate insist that it was one of the best things they ever did, not only because of the volunteering they do, but also because of the support system and immediate group of friends.

The College Prowler® Grade on
Greek Life: C+

A high grade in Greek Life indicates that sororities and fraternities are not only present, but also active on campus. Other determining factors include the variety of houses available and the respect the Greek community receives from the rest of the campus.

Drug Scene

The Lowdown On...
Drug Scene

Most Prevalent Drugs on Campus:
Alcohol
Marijuana

Liquor-Related Referrals:
222

Liquor-Related Arrests:
0

Drug-Related Referrals:
16

Drug-Related Arrests:
16

Drug Counseling Programs

The Chemical Awareness Program (CAP)

An eight-hour educational/awareness program for students who violate campus alcohol and other drug policies. It may also be used by students who wish to learn more about their use/abuse patterns.

EMPOWER

A peer education group that provides alcohol and other drug awareness and refusal skill building.

Students Speak Out On...
Drug Scene

> "The College's drug scene is lively, but not prominent. It's all about knowing the right people and going to the right parties."

Q "I don't know if there are any drugs in Wooster. I'm sure it's here, but if it is, **it's not a big problem**."

Q "Sometimes, you get a whiff of pot, but **by no means are drugs a major player** at Wooster."

Q "**Drugs aren't a problem**, but if you want something, you can probably find it. You don't have to do drugs to have fun."

Q "**Everyone uses drugs,** mostly marijuana. I used to know a guy whose roommate had an opium den in their room, but that was a couple years ago."

Q "Let's just say that you know it's there, but **you don't really ever see it**."

Q "Drugs exist, just like anywhere else, but they aren't really big at all on this campus; if it is big, it's mostly marijuana. I have never seen any drugs on campus, but **I know they're around**."

Q "The kids that do drugs heavily **don't last a second** at Wooster."

Q "Although I have never experienced drugs, I know that the **most popular one is marijuana**. Other than that, I have no idea."

Q "It's not my scene, so I don't know anything about it. **It doesn't seem to be a problem**, though, or I would hear more about it. "

Q "I don't do drugs. I know a few people on campus who do. I don't know how they get it, but they always do. Be careful heading out to the Holden lot, **you're bound to get a contact buzz**."

The College Prowler Take On...
Drug Scene

Drugs at Wooster are there, treading below the surface of student activity, but they are reasonably hard to find. Marijuana is probably the hardest drug out here. There are certain places you know where to look, and the Crandalls (the hippie fraternity) are sure to be able to hook you up if you need them, but for people who don't smoke, it's a non-issue.

Probably the most commonly used drug on campus is alcohol, and sometimes, Red Bull or another energy drink mixed with alcohol, which is never a good idea. Drugs may not be hard to find on campus, but they also aren't used by many, and the drug scene is miniscule.

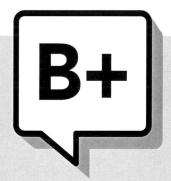

The College Prowler® Grade on

Drug Scene: B+

A high grade in the Drug Scene indicates that drugs are not a noticeable part of campus life; drug use is not visible, and no pressure to use them seems to exist.

Campus Strictness

The Lowdown On...
Campus Strictness

What Are You Most Likely to Get Caught Doing on Campus?

- Drinking underage
- Open cans or cups outside at night
- Smoking pot
- Stealing food from Lowry
- Parking illegally
- Disrupting quiet hours
- Having candles in your room
- Having a microwave in your room
- Having sex on top of McGaw Chapel
- Sneaking into the tunnels

Students Speak Out On...
Campus Strictness

"I've never been caught, but I hear stories all the time about people being caught in someone else's room with a beer in front of them, and security will charge them even though they aren't holding it."

Q "I guess we're strict, but I'm not that sure. **I've never been caught**. Well, there was one time my friends and I escaped from security, and they had an all-points bulletin out for us, but we weren't caught."

Q "The campus is pretty strict when the offender is caught. If it goes to the Judicial Board **they look at past offenses**, but try to first help the student and the campus community."

Q "**It seems to be pretty strict at Wooster**, so don't be so obvious that you get caught with it."

Q "**Just follow the law**; it's as simple as that."

Q "**They're pretty strict**. Every party I've been to so far they have showed up."

Q "**I'm always caught with food**. Sometimes I try to sneak past Rose and Georgia at the swipe counter, but half the time they see the napkin-wrapped food in my hand, and they always make a big deal about it, so my friends have to change my clothing and hair and sneak the food out for me."

Q "It depends. I think security is really strict about drugs and alcohol and stuff, but **there are some rules that everyone breaks**, like having microwaves in your room or lighting incense. I mean, heck, my RA last year told us we could use her microwave if we wanted to!"

Q "**Don't be stupid** with the drinking, and you're alright."

Q "This campus is so strict. I swear, I think security has contests to see **who can write the most alcohol tickets**."

Q "Don't know. I've heard stories but haven't ever been caught. **Security tries to be all tough**, and the RAs are forced to be tough, too, but some don't care. My RA this year is all about pretending we are all 21. I drink with him all the time."

Q "I've seen many an **alcohol ticket** written."

Q "Not very strict at all. An alcohol ticket is like **a slap on the wrist**. It just bums people out a lot."

The College Prowler Take On...
Campus Strictness

While students were quick to say strict, not many could actually think of a time when they had been caught. Like the drugs that float around campus, alcohol tickets are given out with just slightly more frequency. Sure, stories travel fast, but they are few and far between. Students think the College may have a very good system going—give a few alcohol tickets all at once and you've warned the entire campus.

If you are drunk, but not currently drinking, security is usually more interested in making sure that you are properly taken care of than busting you and your friends. Watch out for stealthy police from the town, however. They will try and bust you for carrying empty cups around on the street at night, and they are not pleasant to deal with. Above all, just behave reasonably with alcohol. If you turn around with a beer and see a security guard directly behind you, don't give him the deer-caught-in-headlights look; remain calm and pretend the cup in your hand lives there all the time. If they enter a room you are in, try to move the cup to the floor or out of your hand, preferably, but don't stand by it, and don't be obvious!

D+

The College Prowler® Grade on

Campus Strictness: D+

A high Campus Strictness grade implies an overall lenient atmosphere; police and RAs are fairly tolerant, and the administration's rules are flexible.

Parking

The Lowdown On...
Parking

Student Parking Lot?
Yes

Freshmen Allowed to Park?
Yes

Approximate Parking Permit Cost:
$75 per semester
$150 full year

Wooster Parking Services:
(330) 287-2590
www.wooster.edu/security

Common Parking Tickets:
Without A Permit: $100
No Parking Zone: $50
Handicapped Zone: $100
Fire Lane: $50
Other Violations: $25

Parking Permits

Parking at Wooster is on a first-come, first-serve basis. There are roughly 700 spaces all over campus for students, and the older you are, the better your chances of not getting shut out.

Did You Know?

Best Places to Find a Parking Spot:

The lot behind Westminster house, the lot behind Monyer and Security, by the stadium, and behind the communication building

Good Luck Getting a Parking Spot Here!

Andrews parking lot, behind Holden, by Kenarden, and the Armington lot

Students Speak Out On...
Parking

"Parking is a pain wherever you go. As they have changed the parking for this year, I do not know the scenario anymore. My suggestion, though, is always get a parking pass right away."

Q "**Parking is horrible**, and I don't even have a car here!"

Q "Even though it's really hard to get a pass, I have a car here, and I like that **I can always go into my lot** this year and find a spot to park. It definitely is nicer than last year."

Q "**It's like a scene from *Friday the 13th***—except the North End Garage is Jason. Parking is beyond scarce."

Q "The parking is so horrible at Wooster. They want you to stay in the little college bubble. There is limited parking, excessive fines, and **they tow your car all the time!**"

Q "**I hate the parking rules that the town has made up**. They have signs all over saying 'No Parking 1 to 6 a.m.', which means that normally streets near the College where kids would park are now places that the police watch. They'll chalk your car tires if your car hasn't moved in a while, and then they will tow it."

Q "**Parking's really expensive**, but it is very convenient if you have the opportunity to get a spot."

Q "I like that the College is listening to us this year and finally got a better system. We play a game at my house. We watch out the back window, and when people park illegally in our lot, we call security and watch them get towed. I know it sounds horrible, but you know what? I paid way too much for that pass to let someone else park there. **Read the signs** and go somewhere else!"

Q "**I just brought my bike**. It is so much more convenient— I can get to it when I want, it's free, many people have them, and I don't waste my time fighting with the school."

Q "I can't begin to comment on parking. It's impossible. **Don't bring a car**."

Q "**Parking is a royal pain**. It's not easy to park, which is why I choose not to bring a car on campus."

Q "I think that this year **it's very interesting how much parking prices have gone up** and how little change there have been in terms of security."

Q "**The parking scene is terrible**. Parking passes are extremely overpriced, and money is made by enforcing the rules. People who are alumni and friends of the College get kicked off because they park in the wrong place, and that leads to bad town relations, of which there is already plenty."

Q "It's not so bad this year. I'm sure we all agree that **the prices are a little on the steep side**, though. I feel bad for the people who couldn't get passes; they have to find illegal ones and stuff."

The College Prowler Take On...
Parking

Up until last year, parking on campus was horrendous. Spots were constantly being taken by non-permit holders, students were complaining that they had to park across campus from their dorms, and when the College had weekend events that brought in friends of the College from outside, the complaining upped itself a notch. It didn't help that the neighborhoods around the campus don't want college students parking in front of their houses. The town retaliated and passed some restrictive laws during the 2002-03 school year.

However, this year the complaints department has been noticeably quiet. Students were outraged when they discovered that parking was being raised in price, but they have been pacified by the number of people who have been towed and the ease of finding a space. There have been rumbles about prices, but a quadrants system has been installed, which means that cars can only park in certain areas on campus. Therefore, students will never be across campus and away from the safety of their dorm. It has also been easier to catch offenders.

The College Prowler® Grade on

Parking: C

A high grade in this section indicates that parking is both available and affordable, and that parking enforcement isn't overly severe.

Transportation

The Lowdown On...
Transportation

Ways to Get Around Town:

On Campus
Walk

Ride a community bike

Public Transportation
None. The College provides weekend shuttles or buses to off-campus events.

Taxi Cabs
Miller Cab
629 Nold Ave.
(330) 622-8294

Car Rentals
Alamo, local: (330) 262-7280;
national: (800) 327-9633,
www.alamo.com

Avis,
national: (800) 831-2847,
www.avis.com

Enterprise,
local: (330) 264-1212;
national: (800) 736-8222,
www.enterprise.com

Hertz,
national: (800) 654-3131,
www.hertz.com

National,
national: (800) 227-7368,
www.nationalcar.com

Best Ways to Get Around Town

Borrow a campus bike

Borrow a friend's car

Ride a bike

Walk

Ways to Get Out of Town:

Airlines Serving Cleveland

American Airlines,
(800) 433-7300,
www.americanairlines.com

Continental,
(800) 523-3273,
www.continental.com

Delta,
(800) 221-1212,
www.delta-air.com

Northwest,
(800) 225-2525,
www.nwa.com

Southwest,
(800) 435-9792,
www.southwest.com

TWA,
(800) 221-2000,
www.twa.com

United,
(800) 241-6522,
www.united.com

US Airways,
(800) 428-4322,
www.usairways.com

Airport

Cleveland Hopkins
International Airport

5300 Riverside Dr.
Cleveland, OH 44135

(216) 265-6030

How to Get to the Airport

Cab (A cab ride to the airport costs about $90.)

College shuttles
(Call Lowry for shuttle information—times alternate for holidays.)

Directions

- First, take Burbank Rd/OH-83. Continue to follow OH-83 for 11 miles.

- Then merge onto I-71 N for 35 miles. Take I-480 W via exit 238 toward I-480 W/Airport/Toledo.

- After that, take the OH-237 S exit/Exit 10 toward the Airport exit. Turn left onto Park Rd.

- Turn slight left to take the long-term parking ramp, then turn left onto Hotel Rd.

Greyhound

781 Grant St.
Akron, OH 44311

(330) 434-9185

Amtrak

906 E Bowery St.
Akron, OH 44308

(877) 632-3788

Travel Agents

AAA Travel Agency

2873 Cleveland Rd.
Wooster, OH 44691

(330) 345-5550

VIP Travel of Wooster Inc

2200 Benden Dr. # 1
Wooster, OH 44691

(800) 232-6000
(330) 264-5554

Students Speak Out On...
Transportation

> **"There is no community public transportation. The College sets up a bus system every other weekend or so to the hot spots around town, but other than that, there's nothing."**

Q "It's not that convenient. There are no buses or anything in Wooster. **The school shuttles are few and far between.**"

Q "The town isn't that big, and **there isn't transportation.** That's when you get a friend to drive you."

Q "**Public transportation**? In Wooster? There isn't any."

Q "**I've never used it.** There was the bus coming back from Bacch, but it would only take you to the College."

Q "Man, **the lack of public transportation here has me bummed out.** It sucks!"

Q "Does Wooster have public transportation? **I've never seen any**, but it must exist around here somewhere."

Q "**There's no bus system**, but the College has shuttles that run to the different ends of town on the weekends. From what I hear, they are on time and they are pretty efficient."

Q "Most things are **close enough to walk to**; there isn't real public transportation."

Q "Why would you need transportation? **Where are you going to go**? Drug Mart? Let me hop on the bus for 30 seconds please. Public transportation doesn't exist in Wooster for a good reason—it is not necessary!"

The College Prowler Take On...
Transportation

What transportation? Wooster does not have public transportation. It is completely unnecessary. If you need to get anywhere, you can walk, ride your bike, or ride someone else's bike. Wooster is a town of 26,000 people and 200,000 cows. If you ever find yourself in the position of needing to get to Wal-Mart and it's 11 p.m. and no shuttles are offered at that time, your best bet is to go and beg a friend or stranger for the use of their car. If you aren't in dire need to get whatever it is you want at 11 p.m., just wait; in the morning you will undoubtedly find a poor sap to take you.

You may also want to try bartering with people. Some college students will let you do anything for a free $6 pizza (or anything else for $6).

The College Prowler® Grade on

Transportation: D

A high grade for Transportation indicates that campus buses, public buses, cabs, and rental cars are readily-available and affordable. Other determining factors include proximity to an airport and the necessity of transportation.

Weather

The Lowdown On...
Weather

Average Temperature:

Fall:	52 °F
Winter:	28 °F
Spring:	50 °F
Summer:	71 °F

Average Precipitation:

Fall:	3.00 in.
Winter:	2.30 in.
Spring:	3.38 in.
Summer:	4.01 in.

Students Speak Out On...
Weather

> "Weather varies in Ohio. Bring sweaters, because it can get quite windy, but it is so hard to tell with Northeast Ohio. Be prepared for anything, warm and cold."

Q "It's gray for six straight months, but **the snow is fun**."

Q "**We get all four seasons**—summer, spring, winter, and fall. Wooster has everything. Heavy snow, unbearable heat, murky rain."

Q "The weather is all over the place, but we don't get too much snow. **Bring a lot of different clothes**."

Q "The weather is typical of the Midwest with hot summers, cold winters, and unpredictable falls and springs. **Expect snow**—sometimes lots, sometimes little. Bring very adaptable clothing (layers are a good bet)."

Q "**It's very gray**. Bring hot weather clothes for the first and last weeks of the school year and then warmer clothes for the rest."

Q "It's Ohio. **Bring clothing for all seasons**."

Q "**Ohio weather is spontaneous**. Bring a good sweatshirt when you move in, and bring your fall/winter clothes after fall break. Don't pack too many clothes. You won't wear them all and you know it. You will need a good winter coat come December."

Q "It is freezing! **Bring lots of warm stuff**, because it is only September, and I am already cold."

Q "It often rains or snows here. **It can get cold, very cold**. Bring warm clothes."

Q "**The weather is simple**. Wooster has four seasons— winter, spring, fall, and summer. Just be prepared for hot days in the months typically thought of as hot and cold days in the months typically thought of as cold."

Q "Hot in the fall, freezing in the winter. **Bring your entire wardrobe**. We get all four seasons."

The College Prowler Take On...
Weather

Weather in Ohio can be somewhat of a shock if you hail from places like Texas. Wooster students experience very hot temperatures in the summer (the average feels more like 80°F) and very cold temperatures in the winter that make you shiver to your bones. People will tell you that the weather is wacky in Ohio, and they are right. The seasons seem to change on a whim. One minute it will be 75 degrees outside, and the humidity will make the sweat drip off your face, the next day it will be 57 degrees, and you'll need to bring out the long sleeves. That's Indian summer for you. The good thing is that you don't need your fan in the spring, only at the beginning of the fall. Since classes end the first week of May, the weather is still just pleasant and springy. The heat doesn't choke you until June.

Students should try and dress appropriately, hence not wearing a sweatshirt as your winter coat, and when October hits, pull out the socks and a pair of real shoes. Short skirts in the snow are a bad idea as well. As your mother would say when you were young, "Don't forget your gloves and hat before you go out!"

The College Prowler® Grade on
Weather: C+

A high Weather grade designates that temperatures are mild and rarely reach extremes, that the campus tends to be sunny rather than rainy, and that weather is fairly consistent rather than unpredictable.

Report Card Summary

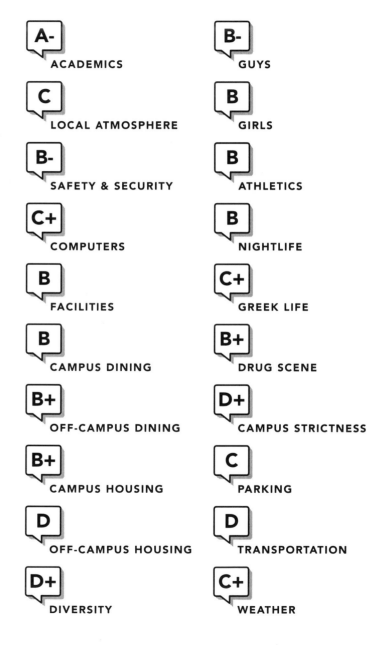

A-
ACADEMICS

B-
GUYS

C
LOCAL ATMOSPHERE

B
GIRLS

B-
SAFETY & SECURITY

B
ATHLETICS

C+
COMPUTERS

B
NIGHTLIFE

B
FACILITIES

C+
GREEK LIFE

B
CAMPUS DINING

B+
DRUG SCENE

B+
OFF-CAMPUS DINING

D+
CAMPUS STRICTNESS

B+
CAMPUS HOUSING

C
PARKING

D
OFF-CAMPUS HOUSING

D
TRANSPORTATION

D+
DIVERSITY

C+
WEATHER

Overall Experience

Students Speak Out On...
Overall Experience

"Overall, Wooster, like any other college, is what you make out of it. I have found warm, friendly people around every corner, professors who are accommodating and approachable, and facilities that are clean and, for the most part, pretty adequate."

Q "The reason I came to Wooster was because of my first visit, I felt comfortable—like I belonged. Now, reflecting on my years spent here, I have been able to grow, get involved, and truly feel like I have made a difference on campus and in the community. Because of Wooster, **I have priceless memories to always look back on**. These reasons are why I first came here, and that's why I'm leaving here happy."

Q "I love Wooster because of Lowry wraps for dinner, and because my friends are here, and we sing, and because my dorm room is huge, and **I love Wooster because of the sidewalks and trees**."

Q "**Wooster was not my first choice**, but I'm glad I am here. I have already been challenged in ways I would have only dreamed of in high school. Of course, that is part of the college experience, but there is just something unique about Wooster."

Q "I love Wooster in the fall, the brightly colored leaves and the light breeze when we're practicing on the field. I've found all of my best friends at Wooster freshman year— friendships that will surely extend beyond graduation. And although IS seems like such a big project, I am actually having fun doing it. **I like researching my topic**—one that I'm genuinely interested in."

Q "I love Wooster mostly because of the people. This has to be one of the greatest schools on earth when it comes to people. The professors are mostly fabulous, friendly, and helpful. And, as for the students, I'll just say **I have more friends here than I've had in my life**!"

Q "Wooster is a good school if you are looking for a small school that allows you to focus heavily on your academics. I enjoy it for that reason. **Sometimes, I wish I had chosen a larger school** for a better social scene and more diversity, but the academics here are top-notch."

Q "I love Wooster. **I love getting to know people so well** and creating a great rapport with my professors. I know that I made the right decision by attending Wooster, and I would never change it. Wooster has been a fabulous part of my life."

Q "Everyday of my life, I wish I was somewhere else. Wooster would be great if it was in a big city, but it is too isolated for my tastes. Plus, **I think it's way too expensive**."

Q "**I absolutely love Woo!** As a member of the swim team and a math major, I have done more here and tried more new things than I would have anywhere else."

Q "Wooster, after several years, has come to mean things that I never could have anticipated—wonderful things. Wooster means waving 'hullo' to people on the way to class that you don't even really know, but you've seen on that route everyday and now consider them a part of your life. **Wooster means running around in the freezing cold, with 100 other students**, stuffing the Kauke Arch with snow for no good reason, but having a marvelous time doing so. Wooster means walking into Mom's Truckstop with the intent of getting a grilled cheese to go, and instead running into an old friend, plopping down and watching him perform card tricks for the next hour. Wooster is a hundred different undefinable things, a crazy world unto itself, a world which I am incredibly grateful and amused to be a part of."

Q "I guess I like Wooster because of the small community. You get a lot of attention from professors. I also love Wooster because **they steal massive amounts of my money for the food plan**, and they take away my computers in the residence halls to give me the Wired Scot. Other than that, there are lots of opportunities for students to get involved in the campus community, and I think there is a lot of diversity on campus. There are a lot of international students and minority students. There are a lot of resources, such as the writing center, that can help students. They helped me! And I have my friends."

Q "As much complaining as I do, I wouldn't rather be anywhere else. I love Wooster. I feel that **I've made some amazing friends** and have gotten a great education."

Q "**Some things could definitely be better**, but I am also getting one of the best college experiences. Wooster has been a great environment for me, but I'm looking forward to living in a big city again after graduation!"

Q "**I love Wooster's unique spirit and traditions**. It's not at every college where you can find bagpipers, a Scottish marching band, Wooster brick paths, and students who participate in everything the school has to offer. Wooster truly is an exciting school with people who care about it. I love when you can walk on a campus, and I know that the people going there love their school."

The College Prowler Take On...
Overall Experience

Here's a news flash—the College of Wooster isn't perfect; you can't please everybody. However, in asking students how they honestly felt about Wooster, even if there are things that they can't stand about the school—things that drive them up the wall, frankly—Wooster students are very glad they chose to come to this college above any other. They say that it's something about the atmosphere, something about the personal touches you see all over campus, and something about the friendships you make here that does it for them. They know that they are receiving a great education that will last them far into their future careers, forming friendships that may last longer than even their marriages, gaining a wonderful background for becoming a richer person, and living life to its fullest.

When a college cares about you the person, not just you the student, or you the number, that is when it becomes more than just a college—it becomes a place you can call home. Wooster has shown that to their students even after graduation, even for decades to come. This is the reason why Wooster students wouldn't trade their years there for anything.

The Inside Scoop

The Lowdown On...
The Inside Scoop

Wooster Slang:

Know the slang, know the school. The following is a list of things you really need to know before coming to Wooster. The more of these words you know, the better off you'll be.

Bacch – Short for Bacchanalia. A huge party with 80-plus kegs that is hosted in Beck's Family Campground every year. People under 21 are allowed in, but are not supposed to drink.

Beast – Milwaukee's Best beer, very cheap and often at large keg parties.

The Cock – Babcock Hall.

COW Card – Wooster students' college ID cards, which are used for everything from the meal plan to printing costs to laundry, and as a debit card.

Cow tipping – The pushing of a sleeping cow until they tip over.

Crandalls – A fraternity that has been underground since the '60s. They sponsor Bacchanalia every year.

The Fishbowl – An area in Lowry dining hall that is separated from the main part by floor to ceiling windows, thereby giving a certain "fishbowl" effect to the area.

Gallows – A 'Who's Line Is It Anyway?' type show run by the chem-free group on campus that holds weekly shows at secret times, so only people with verbal invites can go.

Greenhouse – The environmental student house on campus that is known for its great parties.

Holden Hotel – The newly renovated part of Holden Hall.

Huetters/Hooters – Bornhuetter Hall, because no one can pronounce the name, and it sort of looks mammary.

Kitt – Kittredge Dining Hall.

K-Town – Kenarden Lodge.

Odd Lots – A nickname for Big Lots, a discount bulk store.

PEC – The Armington Physical Education Center.

The Pot – The nickname of the *Potpourri*, a bi-weekly newsletter that sits on the dining hall tables.

The Schwag – Wagner Hall.

Suicide Single – Certain singles in Armington and Stevenson that are two feet smaller than a white-collar jail cell.

Stan the Man – Affectionate nickname of Wooster's President, R. Stanton Hales, who reminds students of a jovial grandfather.

The Twins – Another reference to female anatomy applied to Bornhuetter Hall.

The UG – A nickname for the College Underground, the college club/bar on campus.

The Virgin Vault – Compton, the all-female dorm.

Wally World – A nickname for Wal-Mart.

Woo Goggles – Like beer goggles, it's the effect of the guys or girls around you growing more attractive over a certain span of time. However, the difference with Woo Goggles is that it occurs while sober.

Things I Wish I Knew Before Coming to Wooster

- Everyone's nervous when they first go to college.
- How wonderful the Wooster library is for renting videos.
- The value of personal time—away from roommates, friends, school, and not thinking of anyone but yourself.
- How easy it is to get involved and take on a leadership role.
- Having a campus job rocks!
- Not to get involved in a serious dating relationship the first semester, because there is so much else to experience.
- To transfer as many credits as possible.
- That you need to branch away from your roommate.
- How fun it can be living in a small town and how many cute places are around here that nobody knows about.
- How much I'd miss it when I leave.

Tips to Succeed at Wooster

- Concentrate on your studies your freshman and sophomore years, because things get harder as you get older.
- Go abroad and experience another culture.
- Research your professors before choosing your classes.
- Actually go to class.
- Participate in a lot of activities around campus.
- Have a good work ethic.
- Take time out to develop things you enjoy, not just things you are obligated to do.
- Have fun!

Wooster Urban Legends

- One tradition that has taken on nearly mythical proportions is the filling of Kauke Arch with snow. The rumor is that if Kauke Arch is packed to the very tip-top with snow, classes will be cancelled the next day. Well, whether classes are cancelled or not, the activity is a thrilling nighttime event that students say unites them in a powerful way.

- The president doesn't live in the campus house, but really has a house on Quimby Avenue, even though the College insists that he doesn't.

- A complete network of steam tunnels provides an underground way to get around the whole campus.

- There is a ghost in the attic of Compton who killed herself after not getting into Harvard for grad school. She screams and wails all the time.

- *Playboy* ranked Wooster girls as some of the ugliest girls in America.

- Students pay $31,300 a year to go here. No one pays that much, they all have scholarships or financial aid.

School Spirit

People at Wooster talk fondly about everything, from the kilts to the bagpipes and more. Seniors say that when they walk along to class and hear the thin whistle of bagpipes from across campus, they get prickles in their eyes. Underclassmen even agree that they love the common thread that holds students together at Wooster—they chose this college, for better or for worse—and it shows in every activity they do. Whether it is cheering for the football team or helping out with the recycling crew, Wooster students jump in wholeheartedly.

Traditions

The Arch

The Delmar Archway, or "the Arch" as it is more commonly known, was constructed during the 1961–62 renovation of Kauke Hall. Kauke Hall is the most recognizable building on campus, and the Arch is the reason why. Students are introduced to the Arch when they first arrive on campus. First-year students gather in front of the Arch for their class picture as soon as they arrive on campus, and then they are led by the Scot Pipers through the Arch into McGaw Chapel where they are welcomed by President Hales. Graduating seniors march through the Arch before being seated in the Oak Grove for the start of Commencement ceremonies. When they return for their class reunions, they will march through the Arch again as part of the Parade of Classes.

Bricks

Bricks have become a symbol for the College of Wooster with brick pathways intersecting the different parts of campus. For years, the brick paths were made with bricks manufactured at the Wooster Brick Yards in town. These bricks were marked with the words "Wooster, Ohio." Since bricks are no longer made at the Wooster Brick Yards, these particular bricks have become scarcer as time has gone on, and in turn, are now collector's items to many Wooster loyalists. Students used to steal them from the pathways, but deterred by the lowering number of bricks available, many now sneak out to the dump to get their very own Wooster brick. And the story is, if you steal one before your senior year, you won't graduate!

Kilts

The Scot Band uniforms are one of the most recognized symbols of the College of Wooster. The idea of using a Scottish-style uniform came in the late 1930s while trying to develop a new band uniform. Through a generous donation by alumnus Birt Babcock, the school purchased the first shipment of MacLeod tartan kilts. The MacLeod tartan had no special significance at the time, other than that the tartan matched school colors.

(Kilts, continued)
However, those first kilts did not make it from Scotland. In 1939, that fateful first shipment of kilts was sunk in the Atlantic by a German submarine. Another shipment did make the journey across the Atlantic, and in 1940, the kilts made their debut.

IS March

The IS March is the climax of the IS process that all seniors complete in order to graduate. Each student works with a single faculty member (or two if the student has a double major) on an IS project during most of the senior academic year. The final IS paper or project must be handed in to the Registrar by 4 p.m. the first Monday after Spring Break, which is usually at the end of March. Whether the project is handed in at the last minute or completed a month earlier, seniors who complete the IS process can participate in the IS March, which kicks off at 5 p.m. that same Monday. The March starts at the Kauke Arch and proceeds around campus. During that time, students show their excitement in a number of different ways. The March ends at Kittredge Dining Hall where dinner and an awards ceremony take place. Among the honors given are prizes for the longest and shortest IS titles.

The Rock

The "Wooster Rock" was given by the class of 1874, and during the past 125 years, it has carved its place in Wooster history. In 1873, the graduating class planted a memorial tree. Unfortunately, a passing cow disapproved of the tree and made short work of it. The class of 1874 wanted something that would stand the test of time and wandering cows. Upon the suggestion of Dr. ON Stoddard, professor of natural sciences, the class of 1874 removed the rock laboriously from a site near the present Westminster Church House. The rock is the remaining link to Wooster's earlier days as it was placed just south of Old Main, which was leveled by a fire on December 11, 1901.

(The Rock, continued)

In 1971, the 20-ton rock was sinking into the ground, so it was moved about 40 feet to its current location where it sits next to McGaw Chapel on a 15-ton base of gravel and concrete. The rock has become a notable landmark as it has been painted red, blue, and in stripes; at least one attempt was made to dynamite it. During the 50th reunion for the class of 1874, William Pocock, the class secretary, stated "[the rock] has heard so many confessions of lovers, and is in possession of so many secrets, that it now commands the respect of all."

Scot Pipers

Since the early days of the Scot Band, which performed for the first time in 1940, there were pipers, but it was not until 1962 that there was a serious attempt to organize and train a pipe band with dancers. The band has traditionally appeared at home football games and at some away games. The sight of the Scot Pipers as they march over the hill and into the football stadium is one that alumni rank among their fondest memories of Wooster. In addition to their popular performances with the Scot Marching Band at football games, the Pipers perform at fairs, dinners, parties, and churches during the school year. On campus, their appearances are not limited to the football field. They often lead the basketball teams onto the floor, and more recently, they began escorting the graduating class into the Oak Grove at the start of Commencement ceremonies.

Tootsie Rolls

Each year when seniors turn their Independent Study projects in to the registrar, they receive a miniature Tootsie Roll as a prize. The Tootsie Roll custom began about 20 years ago when one of the College's registrars thought it would be a nice gesture to give students something in return for their work on the IS projects. Why Tootsie Rolls? It just so happened that the registrar got a good deal on bulk Tootsie Rolls! While it may seem like a trivial thing, more than a few Wooster alumni have had their pieces of candy bronzed for posterity.

Finding a Job or Internship

The Lowdown On...
Finding a Job or Internship

The Rubbermaid Career Services Center is the College's best-kept secret. Senior year, when students are frustrated by classes, IS, GREs, and MCATs, they make one last, final gasp for help in sorting out their future by going to the center. And they are amazed by what they find. The Career Services Center offers a plethora of help to students who are looking for internships and future jobs, and students highly suggest visiting them before you graduate.

Advice
Don't wait until your senior year. Go to the Career Services building as soon as you get onto campus. They will help you figure out what you want to do with the rest of your life through things like the Meyers-Briggs personality test, personal career advising and assessments, a wide alumni network, and much, much more.

Career Center Resources & Services

Career Advising

Career Assessments

The Career Library

Career Workshops & Seminar

E-recruiting at *http://wooster.erecruiting.com*

Graduate and Professional School Advising and Information

Interview Practice

Recruitment/Job Fairs

Scots Career Network (assess to alumni)

Grads Entering the Job Market Within
6 Months: 90%
1 Year: N/A

Firms that Most Frequently Hire Graduates

United Way, American Express, Peace Corps, various educational institutions, Americorps

Alumni

The Lowdown On...
Alumni

Web Site:
http://alumni.wooster.edu

Office:
Office of Alumni Relations
Gault Alumni Center
1189 Beall Ave.
Wooster, Ohio 44691
(330) 263-2324
Fax: (330) 263-2250
E-Mail: alumni@wooster.edu

Services Available

Gault Alumni Center is located on the south end of campus across from Luce Hall. The building housed the Department of Music from 1941 until 1987, and bore the name of Karl Merz, the first director of Wooster's Conservatory of Music (1882-1890). From 1987 until 1992, it served as a residence for students. Generous gifts from alumni in the 50-year reunion classes of 1936, 1938, 1940, and 1941, as well as a major contribution from Mr. and Mrs. Gault, made it possible to renovate the building completely during the 1992-93 academic years to serve as a home for the Alumni Association and for use by the Alumni and Development Offices. It contains two large parlors/sitting areas, a meeting room, a main desk, a kitchen, and several offices throughout the building. It is open from 9 a.m. to 5 p.m., Monday through Friday.

Major Alumni Events

Two of the largest alumni events are Homecoming, which is held in the fall during a major rival home game, and Alumni Weekend, which is an annual event held during the summer for those class years who are celebrating a reunion.

Alumni Publications

Wooster Magazine is a quarterly magazine for alumni and friends of the college that is sent out, free of charge, to approximately 28,000 alumni.

Did You Know?

Wooster On-line has an **e-mail newsletter**.

Student Organizations

Visit any of these organizations Web sites at: *www.wooster.edu/home/Student_Activities.php*.

Academic

Archaeology Student Colloquium

The Art Club

Chemistry Club

Communications Club

Geology Club

Jenny Investment Club

Model United Nations

National Student, Speech, Hearing, Language Assoc.

Philosophy Club

Physics Club

Pursuing Scientific Interests

Student Mathematics Association of America

VIEW (Visions in Education at Wooster)

Honorary

Eta Sigma Phi

Lambda Pi Eta

Phi Alpha Theta

Phi Beta Kappa

Psi Chi

Governing Bodies

Campus Council

Inter-Greek Council

Judicial Board

Student Government Association

Religious

Fellowship of Christian Athletes

Hillel

Koinonia

Muslim Student Association

Newman Catholic Student Association

Sisters in Spirit

Wooster Christian Fellowship

Wooster Interfaith Housing

Word Up! Bible Study

Arts and Culture

COW Belles Female a cappella Group

Dance Company

Don't Throw Shoes

Let's Dance

Merry Kuween of Skots Male a cappella group

Scot Marching/Symphonic Band

Scot Pipers

Student Activities Board

Student Music Association

Wooster African Drum & Dance

Wooster Scottish Arts Society

Recreation & Sports

Badminton Club/Table Tennis Club

Men's Club Volleyball

Personal Foul Dance Team

Rampant COW Ultimate Frisbee

Scot Cheerleaders

Women's Athletic & Recreation Association

WOODS

Wooster Cricket Club

Service Groups

Boy's Village

COW 4 Kids

Circle K

Every Woman's House

Forever Young

Goodwill

Habitat for Humanity

Opportunity School

Wooster Volunteer Network

The YMCA

Special Interest

Allies & Queers

Amnesty International

College Democrats

College Republicans

Common Grounds

COW Jugglers

Dene House

ECOS

EMPOWER

Green House

Lighthouse

Wooster Medieval Society

The Best
& Worst

The Ten **BEST** Things About Wooster

1. Small classes
2. The great community
3. Bagpipes
4. Filling the Arch with snow
5. The dorm rooms
6. Strong academic programs
7. The spring
8. Diversity
9. The professors
10. The lifelong friends made here

The Ten **WORST** Things About Wooster

1 No 24-hour food places

2 The crazy Ohio weather

3 The dorm rooms

4 useIT (The computer people)

5 The PEC

6 Stevenson Hall

7 Boy/girl ratio

8 E-mail on virus kicks

9 The townies screaming things out of their cars

10 The construction

Visiting

The Lowdown On...
Visiting

Hotel Information:

AmeriHost East

2055 Lincoln Way, E US 30
Wooster, OH 44691

(330) 262-5008

Distance from Campus:
2.34 miles

Price Range: $64–$119

AmeriHost North

789 E Milltown Rd.
Wooster, OH 44691

(330) 345-1500

Distance from Campus:
2.1 miles

Price Range: $69–$125

**Barrister's End Bed
& Breakfast**

356 N Market St.
Wooster, OH 44691

(330) 262-4085

Distance from Campus: 1 mile

Price Range: $80–$95

➜

Best Western Hotel

243 E Liberty St.
Wooster, OH 44691

(330) 264-7750

www.bestwestern.com

Distance from Campus: 1 mile

Price Range: $59–109

Econo-Lodge

2137 Lincoln Way
Wooster, OH 44691

(330) 264-8883

Distance from Campus:
2.4 miles

Price Range: $60–80

Gasche House Bed & Breakfast

340 N Bever St.
Wooster, OH 44691

(330) 264-8231

Distance from Campus:
0.8 miles

Price Range: $92–$125

Hampton Inn

4253 Burbank Rd.
Wooster, OH 44691

(330) 345-4424 or
(800) 426-7866

Distance from Campus:
3.1 miles

Price Range: $75–125

Leila Belle Inn

846 E Bowman St.
Wooster, OH 44691

(Seasonal, April — October)

(330) 262-8866

Distance from Campus:
0.7 miles

Price Range: $134–$184

Mirabelle Bed & Breakfast

1626 Beall Ave.
Wooster, OH 44691

(330)264-6006 or
(800) 294-7857

Distance from Campus:
0.5 miles

Price Range: $84–$114

The Wooster Inn

801 E Wayne Ave.
Wooster, OH 44691

(330) 263-2660

Distance from Campus:
0.5 miles

Price Range: $90–$150

Take a Campus Virtual Tour

www.wooster.edu/admissions/campustour/default.php

To Schedule a Group Information Session or Interview

To schedule an appointment with admissions, call their toll-free number, 1-800-877-9905, or schedule an individual visit online at *http://admissions.wooster.edu/admissions/visit/schedule.php.*

Campus Tours

Campus tours are available Monday through Friday from 9 a.m. to 11 a.m. and 1 p.m. to 4 p.m., as well as Saturdays (September through May) from 9 a.m. to 11 a.m. They take place on the hour. Tours are conducted by current students, who will personalize your visit to meet your specific interests. Remember to make your reservations to visit at least one week in advance!

Overnight Visits

Admissions pairs perspectives with a student host for a night. You'll eat in the dining hall, stay in a residence hall, and meet some of the people who make up Wooster. Overnight visits are available on Sunday through Thursday nights, and must be scheduled one week in advance. Overnight visits will not be available from May 2 to September 5. Don't forget your sleeping bag!

Directions to Campus

Driving from the North (Cleveland)

- I-71 S to Rte. 83 (Wooster Exit)

- South on Rte. 83 for 14 miles to Wooster

- Once you enter Wooster, continue on Rte. 83 S

- Take the second exit, which is Rte. 585/Bowman Street

- Turn right onto Bowman Street

- Turn right onto Beall Avenue (3 stop lights)

- Proceed north to Lowry Center

Driving from the South/West (Columbus)

- I-71 N to Rte. 30 E

- Rte. 30 E for 28 miles into Wooster

- Exit onto Madison Avenue

- Turn right off exit and proceed into Wooster on Bever Street

- Turn right on Pine Street

- Turn left onto Beall Avenue (2 blocks)

- Proceed north to Lowry Center

Driving from the East (Akron)

- I-76 W to Rte. 21 S

- Rte. 21 S to Rte. 585

- Rte. 585 W for 22 miles into Wooster

- Rte. 585 W becomes Bowman Street

- Turn right onto Beall Avenue

- Proceed north to Lowry Center

Words to Know

Academic Probation – A suspension imposed on a student if he or she fails to keep up with the school's minimum academic requirements. Those unable to improve their grades after receiving this warning can face dismissal.

Beer Pong/Beirut – A drinking game involving cups of beer arranged in a pyramid shape on each side of a table. The goal is to get a ping pong ball into one of the opponent's cups by throwing the ball or hitting it with a paddle. If the ball lands in a cup, the opponent is required to drink the beer.

Bid – An invitation from a fraternity or sorority to 'pledge' (join) that specific house.

Blue-Light Phone – Brightly-colored phone posts with a blue light bulb on top. These phones exist for security purposes and are located at various outside locations around most campuses. In an emergency, a student can pick up one of these phones (free of charge) to connect with campus police or a security escort.

Campus Police – Police who are specifically assigned to a given institution. Campus police are typically not regular city officers; they are employed by the university in a full-time capacity.

Club Sports – A level of sports that falls somewhere between varsity and intramural. If a student is unable to commit to a varsity team but has a lot of passion for athletics, a club sport could be a better, less intense option. Even less demanding, intramural (IM) sports often involve no traveling and considerably less time.

Cocaine – An illegal drug. Also known as "coke" or "blow," cocaine often resembles a white crystalline or powdery substance. It is highly addictive and dangerous.

Common Application – An application with which students can apply to multiple schools.

Course Registration – The period of official class selection for the upcoming quarter or semester. Prior to registration, it is best to prepare several back-up courses in case a particular class becomes full. If a course is full, students can place themselves on the waitlist, although this still does not guarantee entry.

Division Athletics – Athletic classifications range from Division I to Division III. Division IA is the most competitive, while Division III is considered to be the least competitive.

Dorm – A dorm (or dormitory) is an on-campus housing facility. Dorms can provide a range of options from suite-style rooms to more communal options that include shared bathrooms. Most first-year students live in dorms. Some upperclassmen who wish to stay on campus also choose this option.

Early Action – An application option with which a student can apply to a school and receive an early acceptance response without a binding commitment. This system is becoming less and less available.

Early Decision – An application option that students should use only if they are certain they plan to attend the school in question. If a student applies using the early decision option and is admitted, he or she is required and bound to attend that university. Admission rates are usually higher among students who apply through early decision, as the student is clearly indicating that the school is his or her first choice.

Ecstasy – An illegal drug. Also known as "E" or "X," ecstasy looks like a pill and most resembles an aspirin. Considered a party drug, ecstasy is very dangerous and can be deadly.

Ethernet – An extremely fast Internet connection available in most university-owned residence halls. To use an Ethernet connection properly, a student will need a network card and cable for his or her computer.

Fake ID – A counterfeit identification card that contains false information. Most commonly, students get fake IDs with altered birthdates so that they appear to be older than 21 (and therefore of legal drinking age). Even though it is illegal, many college students have fake IDs in hopes of purchasing alcohol or getting into bars.

Frosh – Slang for "freshman" or "freshmen."

Hazing – Initiation rituals administered by some fraternities or sororities as part of the pledging process. Many universities have outlawed hazing due to its degrading, and sometimes dangerous, nature.

Intramurals (IMs) – A popular, and usually free, sport league in which students create teams and compete against one another. These sports vary in competitiveness and can include a range of activities—everything from billiards to water polo. IM sports are a great way to meet people with similar interests.

Keg – Officially called a half-barrel, a keg contains roughly 200 12-ounce servings of beer.

LSD – An illegal drug, also known as acid, this hallucinogenic drug most commonly resembles a tab of paper.

Marijuana – An illegal drug, also known as weed or pot; along with alcohol, marijuana is one of the most commonly-found drugs on campuses across the country.

Major –The focal point of a student's college studies; a specific topic that is studied for a degree. Examples of majors include physics, English, history, computer science, economics, business, and music. Many students decide on a specific major before arriving on campus, while others are simply "undecided" until declaring a major. Those who are extremely interested in two areas can also choose to double major.

Meal Block – The equivalent of one meal. Students on a meal plan usually receive a fixed number of meals per week. Each meal, or "block," can be redeemed at the school's dining facilities in place of cash. Often, a student's weekly allotment of meal blocks will be forfeited if not used.

Minor – An additional focal point in a student's education. Often serving as a complement or addition to a student's main area of focus, a minor has fewer requirements and prerequisites to fulfill than a major. Minors are not required for graduation from most schools; however some students who want to explore many different interests choose to pursue both a major and a minor.

Mushrooms – An illegal drug. Also known as "'shrooms," this drug resembles regular mushrooms but is extremely hallucinogenic.

Off-Campus Housing – Housing from a particular landlord or rental group that is not affiliated with the university. Depending on the college, off-campus housing can range from extremely popular to non-existent. Students who choose to live off campus are typically given more freedom, but they also have to deal with possible subletting scenarios, furniture, bills, and other issues. In addition to these factors, rental prices and distance often affect a student's decision to move off campus.

Office Hours – Time that teachers set aside for students who have questions about coursework. Office hours are a good forum for students to go over any problems and to show interest in the subject material.

Pledging – The early phase of joining a fraternity or sorority, pledging takes place after a student has gone through rush and received a bid. Pledging usually lasts between one and two semesters. Once the pledging period is complete and a particular student has done everything that is required to become a member, that student is considered a brother or sister. If a fraternity or a sorority would decide to "haze" a group of students, this initiation would take place during the pledging period.

Private Institution – A school that does not use tax revenue to subsidize education costs. Private schools typically cost more than public schools and are usually smaller.

Prof – Slang for "professor."

Public Institution – A school that uses tax revenue to subsidize education costs. Public schools are often a good value for in-state residents and tend to be larger than most private colleges.

Quarter System (or Trimester System) – A type of academic calendar system. In this setup, students take classes for three academic periods. The first quarter usually starts in late September or early October and concludes right before Christmas. The second quarter usually starts around early to mid–January and finishes up around March or April. The last academic quarter, or "third quarter," usually starts in late March or early April and finishes up in late May or Mid-June. The fourth quarter is summer. The major difference between the quarter system and semester system is that students take more, less comprehensive courses under the quarter calendar.

RA (Resident Assistant) – A student leader who is assigned to a particular floor in a dormitory in order to help to the other students who live there. An RA's duties include ensuring student safety and providing assistance wherever possible.

Recitation – An extension of a specific course; a review session. Some classes, particularly large lectures, are supplemented with mandatory recitation sessions that provide a relatively personal class setting.

Rolling Admissions – A form of admissions. Most commonly found at public institutions, schools with this type of policy continue to accept students throughout the year until their class sizes are met. For example, some schools begin accepting students as early as December and will continue to do so until April or May.

Room and Board – This figure is typically the combined cost of a university-owned room and a meal plan.

Room Draw/Housing Lottery – A common way to pick on-campus room assignments for the following year. If a student decides to remain in university-owned housing, he or she is assigned a unique number that, along with seniority, is used to determine his or her housing for the next year.

Rush – The period in which students can meet the brothers and sisters of a particular chapter and find out if a given fraternity or sorority is right for them. Rushing a fraternity or a sorority is not a requirement at any school. The goal of rush is to give students who are serious about pledging a feel for what to expect.

Semester System – The most common type of academic calendar system at college campuses. This setup typically includes two semesters in a given school year. The fall semester starts around the end of August or early September and concludes before winter vacation. The spring semester usually starts in mid-January and ends in late April or May.

Student Center/Rec Center/Student Union – A common area on campus that often contains study areas, recreation facilities, and eateries. This building is often a good place to meet up with fellow students; depending on the school, the student center can have a huge role or a non-existent role in campus life.

Student ID – A university-issued photo ID that serves as a student's key to school-related functions. Some schools require students to show these cards in order to get into dorms, libraries, cafeterias, and other facilities. In addition to storing meal plan information, in some cases, a student ID can actually work as a debit card and allow students to purchase things from bookstores or local shops.

Suite – A type of dorm room. Unlike dorms that feature communal bathrooms shared by the entire floor, suites offer bathrooms shared only among the suite. Suite-style dorm rooms can house anywhere from two to ten students.

TA (Teacher's Assistant) – An undergraduate or grad student who helps in some manner with a specific course. In some cases, a TA will teach a class, assist a professor, grade assignments, or conduct office hours.

Undergraduate – A student in the process of studying for his or her bachelor's degree.

ABOUT THE AUTHOR

I am a senior at the College of Wooster, currently pursuing an English major and communication minor. I am active in many different organizations at college (mainly because I can't say no), including being a DJ for the College's own radio station, WCWS 90.9 FM. I'm also a Web master for the Babcock International Program, a member of the COW Belles, Wooster's beautiful and fabulous female a cappella group, and the cheese and hot dog girl for Circle K (a great volunteer organization). Last, but certainly not least, I like to lose sleep on Wednesday nights as the Managing Editor of the *Wooster Voice*, the College's weekly, student-run newspaper since 1883.

After college, I plan on heading to graduate school to try my hand at the journalism profession, hopefully learning a little along the way. Look for my byline to grace a publication in the near future, whether it's the *New York Times* or Billy Bob's Quarterly Home Canning Magazine. In the meantime, you can e-mail me with any comments, questions, or fun facts at sarahcore@collegeprowler.com

A big thank you goes out to all the people who put up with me during the process of writing this guidebook, including my parents, Gordon, Lois, and Rachel Core, the entire *Voice* staff (including my News Yoda), my roommate Aubrey, who slept through my typing, Montana and his funny friends who like to distract me at 4 a.m. until I put them to work, Wooster's Career Services, Information Technology, the Longbrake Wellness Center, Safety and Security, for bending over backward to help me get the answers I needed, and everyone at College Prowler.

Sarah E. Core
sarahcore@collegeprowler.com

California Colleges

California dreamin'?
This book is a must have for you!

CALIFORNIA COLLEGES
7¼" X 10", 762 Pages Paperback
$29.95 Retail
1-59658-501-3

Stanford, UC Berkeley, Caltech—California is home
to some of America's greatest institutes of higher
learning. *California Colleges* gives the lowdown on 24
of the best, side by side, in one prodigious volume.

New England Colleges

Looking for peace in the Northeast?
Pick up this regional guide to New England!

NEW ENGLAND COLLEGES
7¼" X 10", 1015 Pages Paperback
$29.95 Retail
1-59658-504-8

New England is the birthplace of many prestigious universities, and with so many to choose from, picking the right school can be a tough decision. With inside information on over 34 competive Northeastern schools, *New England Colleges* provides the same high-quality information prospective students expect from College Prowler in one all-inclusive, easy-to-use reference.

Schools of the South

Headin' down south? This book will help you find your way to the perfect school!

SCHOOLS OF THE SOUTH
7¼" X 10", 773 Pages Paperback
$29.95 Retail
1-59658-503-X

Southern pride is always strong. Whether it's across town or across state, many Southern students are devoted to their home sweet home. *Schools of the South* offers an honest student perspective on 36 universities available south of the Mason-Dixon.

Untangling
the Ivy League

The ultimate book for everything Ivy!

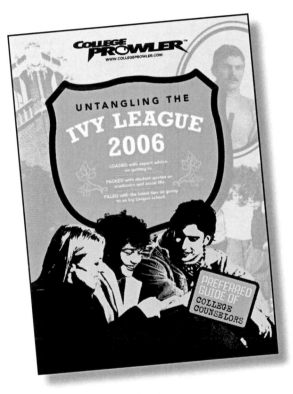

UNTANGLING THE IVY LEAGUE
7¼" X 10", 567 Pages Paperback
$24.95 Retail
1-59658-500-5

Ivy League students, alumni, admissions officers,
and other top insiders get together to tell it like it is.
Untangling the Ivy League covers every aspect—from
admissions and athletics to secret societies and urban
legends—of the nation's eight oldest, wealthiest, and
most competitive colleges and universities.

Tell Us What Life Is Really Like at Your School!

Have you ever wanted to let people know what your college is really like? Now's your chance to help millions of high school students choose the right college.

Let your voice be heard.

Check out *www.collegeprowler.com* for more info!

Need More Help?

Do you have more questions about this school? Can't find a certain statistic? College Prowler is here to help. We are the best source of college information out there. We have a network of thousands of students who can get the latest information on any school to you ASAP. E-mail us at info@collegeprowler.com with your college-related questions.

E-Mail Us Your College-Related Questions!

Check out ***www.collegeprowler.com*** for more details.
1-800-290-2682

Write For Us!
Get published! Voice your opinion.

Writing a College Prowler guidebook is both fun and rewarding; our open-ended format allows your own creativity free reign. Our writers have been featured in national newspapers and have seen their names in bookstores across the country. Now is your chance to break into the publishing industry with one of the country's fastest-growing publishers!

Apply now at *www.collegeprowler.com*

Contact editor@collegeprowler.com or
call 1-800-290-2682 for more details.

Pros and Cons

Still can't figure out if this is the right school for you?
You've already read through this in-depth guide; why not
list the pros and cons? It will really help with narrowing down
your decision and determining whether or not
this school is right for you.

Pros	Cons
....	....
....	....
....	....
....	....
....	....
....	....
....	....
....	....
....	....
....	....
....	....
....	....
....	....

Pros and Cons

Still can't figure out if this is the right school for you?
You've already read through this in-depth guide; why not
list the pros and cons? It will really help with narrowing down
your decision and determining whether or not
this school is right for you.

Pros	Cons
....	....
....	....
....	....
....	....
....	....
....	....
....	....
....	....
....	....
....	....
....	....
....	....

Notes

....
....
....
....
....
....
....
....
....
....
....
....
....
....

Notes

....

....

....

....

....

....

....

....

....

....

....

....

....

Notes

....

....

....

....

....

....

....

....

....

....

....

....

....

....

Notes

....

....

....

....

....

....

....

....

....

....

....

....

....

Notes

....

....

....

....

....

....

....

....

....

....

....

....

....

Notes

....

....

....

....

....

....

....

....

....

....

....

....

....

Notes

....

....

....

....

....

....

....

....

....

....

....

....

....

Notes

....

....

....

....

....

....

....

....

....

....

....

....

....

Notes

....

....

....

....

....

....

....

....

....

....

....

....

....

....

Notes

....

....

....

....

....

....

....

....

....

....

....

....

....

Notes

....

....

....

....

....

....

....

....

....

....

....

....

....